Equality in Law between Men and Women in the European Community

Denmark

Equality in Law between Men and Women in the European Community

Series Editors

MICHEL VERWILGHEN
Professeur ordinaire à la Faculté de Droit
Université catholique de Louvain

FERDINAND VON PRONDZYNSKI
Professor of Law and Dean of the Law School
Jean Monnet Professor of European Social Law
The University of Hull

European Commission

Equality in Law between Men and Women in the European Community

Denmark

by

RUTH NIELSEN
Professor
Law Department
Copenhagen Business School

MARTINUS NIJHOFF PUBLISHERS
THE HAGUE/BOSTON/LONDON

OFFICE FOR OFFICIAL PUBLICATIONS OF THE EUROPEAN COMMUNITIES
LUXEMBOURG

A C.I.P. Catalogue record for this book is available from the Library of Congress.

ISBN (this volume) 0-7923-1830-7 (Martinus Nijhoff Publishers)
92-826-4458-8 (Office for Official Publications of the EC)

This study was commissioned by the Equal Opportunities Unit of Directorate-General V (Employment, Industrial Relations and Social Affairs) of the European Commission. It does not, however, express the Commission's official views. The responsibility for the views expressed lies with the authors.

A French version of this text has been published by the Office for Official Publications of the European Communities and Les Editions Juridiques Bruylant, Brussels.

Published by

Office for Official Publications of the European Communities, L-2985 Luxembourg

ISBN (this volume) 92-826-4458-8 Catalogue number CE-97-92-002-EN-C

and

Kluwer Law International,

P.O. Box 85889, 2508 CN The Hague, The Netherlands

ISBN (series) 0-7923-1842-0 ISBN (this volume) 0-7923-1830-7

Sold and distributed for the Office for Official Publications of the European Communities by the distributors listed on the inside back cover.

Kluwer Law International incorporates the publishing programmes of Graham & Trotman, Kluwer Law & Taxation and Martinus Nijhoff Publishers.

Sold and distributed in the USA and Canada
by Kluwer Academic Publishers,
101 Philip Drive, Norwell, MA 02061, U.S.A.

In all other countries sold and distributed
by Kluwer Academic Publishers Group,
P.O. Box 322, 3300 AH Dordrecht, The Netherlands

Printed in Belgium

TABLE OF CONTENTS

SOURCES OF EQUALITY LAW

FOREWORD

Since the Second World War several international organizations have been endeavouring to promote the principle of equal opportunities between women and men, in law as well as in practice. This objective has also been pursued in a number of countries within the framework of domestic law. The intention has been to pursue a social objective and to achieve a change in the patterns of social conduct. In this context it has been felt that where the law visibly adopts the principle of equality this may contribute to the transformation of attitudes.

It has generally been accepted that equal opportunities ought to be pursued in the working environment in particular. In part this is because employment equality is a concept which can be more easily addressed by legal means than can other aspects of equality, but it is also true that a better distribution of wealth and income between the sexes and the abandonment of separate gender roles in the labour market can provide a powerful impetus to the realization of equal opportunities in society more generally.

To some extent these initiatives have been successful. Progress has been made in a relatively short space of time, although perhaps in limited areas of the equal opportunities agenda. But the impact has been restricted, and much effort still needs to be made in order to improve both law and social practice.

* * *

Within the European Community also there has been a steady growth of interest in the issue of equality between women and men. Article 119 of the Treaty instituting the European Economic Community, signed in Rome on 25 March 1957, provides for equal pay for women and men workers who perform equal work. The main Directive advancing the idea of equal pay, Directive 75/117/EEC, will soon be celebrating its twentieth birthday.

But it is not enough to enact Directives. It is also necessary to analyse and control the implementation of these texts in the Member States of the European Community. The Commission of the European Communities has obviously understood this, since in its Action Programme for 1982-1985 it placed particular emphasis on the need to follow up the implementation of the Equality Directives. In pursuit of this the Commission established a number of expert networks to consider the equality agenda from a variety of viewpoints. One of these networks was the Network of Experts on the Implementation of the Equality Directives, consisting of experts from each of the Member States of the Community.

These experts have drawn up a series of reports on various aspects of their remit, and have been able to offer advice to the Commission on desirable courses of action to be followed. The network has also met regularly to discuss the reports and to update the Commission and each other on important developments in each of the Member States. Some of the network's consolidated reports have been published by the European Commission, and indeed the information contained in network documentation has been used in conferences of legal practitioners and other interested persons organized under the auspices of the Commission. However, the national reports written by network members remain unpublished and are unavailable to the general public.

In fact these reports form an excellent source of legislative and jurisprudential information from the Member States in matters of equality. They shed light on the progress made and the work which remains to be done if we are to achieve equality both in law and in practice. The experts therefore expressed the desire to see their work published and widely disseminated in the European Community and internationally, so that it can be used to assist not only legal practitioners but also other groups and persons seeking to achieve the objective of equal opportunities.

However, the reports drawn up for the network could not necessarily have been published in the form in which they were produced. Their authors had drawn up working documents, rather than studies designed for publication. Furthermore network members were, at any rate initially, given significant discretion as to how the work should be produced. From 1986 onwards a common format based on agreed schemas was devised to give network reports greater homogeneity, and this also prompted a growing desire to produce a more extensive collection of knowledge in this field.

The European Commission therefore decided to promote the progressive publication of an encyclopædia on equality in law between women and men in the European Community. This was to consist of volumes which were no longer to be only administrative documents intended for Commission use, but were to present a high level of scientific and formal quality.

There is no need to discuss at length the importance and interest of such a publication, which forms a natural part of the Commission's programme of action regarding the promotion of equality of opportunity. In fact it represents an excellent method of consolidating Community knowledge of existing legal provisions in order to ensure their better implementation. It represents also the desire to extend and develop the traditional means of disseminating information, in such a way as to sensitize the public more effectively.

The plans for such an encyclopædia were formulated by experts attending the Spanish Presidency seminar on equal opportunities in Toledo in April 1989.

It was with much pleasure that the coordinators of this major project have been able to witness the gradual production of the volumes in this collection. Nevertheless, in spite of all the care take by the experts involved in this work, the encyclopædia is neither exhaustive, perfect nor definitive, since the law continues to evolve. However, it is hoped that it will prove useful to all those — judges, tribunal members, lawyers, civil servants, teachers and researchers — who are interested in this subject.

* * *

The present volume, pertaining to Danish law, is an integral part of the encyclopædia. It was therefore prepared on the basis of a structure common to all volumes in the series, in order to allow for a comparative reading of the law in each Member State on equality between women and men. The volume states the law as at 1 January 1993.

The first part of the volume — the Commentary — is based on a detailed plan common to all the national volumes, drawn up in such a way as to allow the reader to adopt a comparative approach. This plan draws both on the characteristics of the legal systems in use in the States linked to the Roman-Germanic legal tradition, in those following the common law tradition, and in Denmark — the only current Member State in the Nordic tradition. One result of this is that certain headings may not be relevant to the position in each Member State.

The rest of the volume contains legislative texts actually in force in Danish law which implement the principles laid down in the EC Equality Directives, as well as the most significant court and tribunal decisions applying those texts.

* * *

The coordinators wish to express their gratitude to all those who have lent their assistance and support to the encyclopædia project, and to show particular appreciation to certain of them.

We need to record our gratitude to the authors, without whom this work would not have been produced. The essential quality of the encyclopædia lies in the work of its main authors; they spared no effort in the assembling of the necessary documentation and in drawing up an intelligible and useful commentary.

A particular word of thanks is due to the staff of the Equal Opportunities Unit of DG V of the European Commission. Since the project was discussed in the initial stages a large number of officials have been associated with it and have provided active assistance and support to the coordinators. It has been a pleasure to collaborate with the Unit.

Similarly, the coordinators would like to express their sincere thanks to the officials of the Office for Official Publications of the European Communities, whose patient and expert supervision made it possible to convert the manuscripts into publishable texts of a very high quality.

We express particular gratitude to the publishing houses which accepted the burden of the present work, which is hardly lightweight as it numbers some thirty volumes!

May this work assembled with the active participation of so many eminent and committed collaborators contribute to progress in the law, to the common good and to the promotion of formal and actual equality between the women and men of Europe.

Ferdinand von PRONDZYNSKI
Professor of Law and Dean of the Law School
Jean Monnet Professor of European Social Law
The University of Hull
United Kingdom

Michel VERWILGHEN
Professeur ordinaire
à la Faculté de Droit
Université catholique de Louvain
Belgium

NOTICE TO THE READER

The editors of the encyclopædia wish to draw the attention of the reader to certain characteristics of the collection.

1. Each volume of the encyclopædia is published in two languages, English and French. The volumes have been edited so as to ensure that they have, as far as possible, the same content and structure in their English and French versions, although the language and terminology may occasionally differ as a result of normal usage in English and French respectively.

2. The authors of the Commentary section of each volume have worked according to a common schema agreed in the European Commission's Network of Experts on the Implementation of the Equality Directives. This allows the collection as a whole to follow a uniform structure. However, the Sources section in each volume is structured according to the domestic law framework, which varies from Member State to Member State.

3. The materials contained in the Sources section of each volume have (except where the original language is English or French) been translated into the two languages of the encyclopædia. These translations are not official, though every effort has been made to provide translated versions which are of high quality and accuracy. In the event of any doubt, it will be necessary for the reader to refer to legal sources in the original language; these are the only sources of guaranteed accuracy.

4. Equality in law between women and men within the European Community is a subject affected by rapid change, in EC law as well as in the law of each Member State. The formal sources evolve so quickly that information supplied in these volumes may have to be updated from that contained in the published encyclopædia. As far as possible major legislative and jurisprudential changes which occurred during the preparation of the volumes have been indicated in footnotes. The editors hope to be able to produce regular updates at a later stage.

5. References to laws, regulations and judicial decisions follow the normal usage of the Member State from which they originate.

NOTICE TO THE READER

ABBREVIATIONS

[Comments in square brackets are translations or explanations of the relevant Danish expressions or names]

art.(s)	article(s)
A/S	*Aktieselskab* [limited liability company]
CMLR	Common Market Law Reports
DA	*Dansk Arbejdsgiverforening* [Danish Employers' Confederation]
EC	European Community/ies
ECHR	European Convention of Human Rights, or European Court of Human Rights (Strasbourg)
ECJ	European Court of Justice (Luxembourg)
ECR	European Court Reports
EEC	European Economic Community
FTF	*Funktionærernes og Tjenestemændenes Fællesorganisation*
HD	*Højesterets dom* [Supreme Court judgment]
HK	*Handels- og Kontorfunktionærernes Forbund* [Salaried Employees' Union]
ILO	International Labour Organization
KAD	*Kvindeligt Arbejderforbund i Danmark* [Danish Women Workers' Union]
LO	*Landsorganisationen i Danmark* [Federation of Danish Trade Unions]
LP	*Lager- og pakhusarbejdere* [store workers and packers: the name of a section of the trade union SiD, *q.v.*]
Ltd	Limited (liability company)
OJ C	Official Journal of the European Communities, C Series (Information and Notices)
OJ L	Official Journal of the European Communities, L Series (Legislation)
ØLD	*Østre Landsrets dom* [High Court judgment, Eastern Division]
para.(s)	paragraph(s)
Pt	Part
s./ss	section/sections
SHD	*Sø- og Handelsrets dom* [Admiralty and Commercial Court judgment]
SiD	*Specialarbejderforbundet i Danmark* [Danish General Workers' Union]
TFR	*Tidsskrift for Retsvidenskab* [law journal]
U	*Ugeskrift for Retsvæsen* [Danish legal journal, containing law reports]
UN	United Nations
VLD	*Vestre Landsrets dom* [High Court judgment, Western Division]

TABLE OF LEGISLATION ETC.

[Numbers in bold type refer to pages at which provisions are printed verbatim]

Treaties and Conventions

European Communities Secondary Legislation

Statutes

Statutory Instruments

Collective Agreements

TABLE OF CASES

[Numbers in bold type refer to pages at which extracts are printed verbatim]

Numerical Table of Cases before the Court of Justice of the European Communities

Table of Cases Reported in *Ugeskrift for Retsvæsen*

Table of Cases: Supreme Court

Table of Cases: High Court

Table of Cases: Admiralty and Commercial Court

Table of Cases: Arbitration Awards

Table of Cases: Labour Court

Alphabetical Table of Cases

COMMENTARY ON EQUALITY LAW

1. GENERAL

1.1 INTRODUCTION

1.1.1 THE NATIONAL LEGAL SYSTEM

Comparative context

There are major variations[1] between the Member States of the European Community as regards the legal regulation of employment and collective agreements. The 12 Member States can be divided into three groups of labour law tradition:[2]

- nine countries (Germany, France, Belgium, Netherlands, Luxembourg, Spain, Portugal, Italy and Greece) belonging to the Roman-Germanic system;
- two countries (Ireland and the United Kingdom) belonging to the Anglo-Saxon system;
- one country (Denmark) belonging to the Nordic system.

Denmark is, in the EC, the only representative of the Nordic labour law tradition,[3] where there is a stronger emphasis on collective labour law and a weaker protection of individual employment rights than in the other EC countries.

Overview [4]

Danish labour law is traditionally sub-divided into three parts:

- collective labour law;
- individual employment law;
- public labour law.

Collective labour law deals with the rights and duties flowing from collective agreements, which, under Danish law, are legally binding both for

---

1 See Commission of the European Communities, *Summary Report on the Comparative Study on Rules Governing Working Conditions in the Member States*, COM(89) 926, Brussels, 1989.

2 *Ibid.*, Part 1, 'General Aspects'.

3 See N. BRUUN, B. FLODGREN, H. HYDEN, M. HALVORSEN and R. NIELSEN, *Den nordiska modellen. Fackföreningerne och arbetsrätten i Norden*, Malmö, 1989. See also S. EDLUND (ed.), *Labour Law Research in Twelve Countries*, Stockholm, 1986.

4 See R. NIELSEN, 'Danish Labour Law: Research Needs in the 1980s', in S. EDLUND (ed.), *Labour Law Research in Twelve Countries*, Stockholm, 1986.

the parties (organizations) which have concluded them and for members of the parties, that is to say individual workers and individual employers. Individual employment law deals with the rights and duties flowing from the employment contract. Public labour law is the law on the working environment and those parts of social security law which are closely related to the labour market, such as the rules on unemployment and sickness benefit. Major parts of the Danish social security and social welfare system are financed through taxation and are not closely linked to paid employment.

Danish labour has developed through two periods of change and is now, in the 1980s and 1990s, in the midst of a new transformation. In the first phase the formation of the collective labour law system took place. This occurred in Denmark in the late 19th and early 20th centuries. In the second phase, in the period from around 1930 to 1970, the Danish version of the Scandinavian Welfare State was created. In the third and present phase a transformation of the law governing managerial prerogatives is taking place, and Denmark is increasingly being affected by international developments, in particular through the influence of EC law.

The foundation of collective labour law

The strong position of the trade unions may be due to the fact that they, like their other Scandinavian counterparts, adopt a very collaborative attitude towards the employer. The two main organizations on the Danish labour market, the Federation of Trade Unions (*Landsorganisationen i Danmark*: LO) and the Danish Employers' Confederation (*Dansk Arbejdsgiverforening*: DA), concluded a basic agreement, the September Agreement (*Septemberforlig*), in 1899, in which the employers recognized the right of the workers to unionize and the LO in return recognized the managerial prerogatives of employers, in particular the employers' discretionary power in matters of recruitment and dismissal, their right to direct and allocate work, and their right to require supervisors not to join the unions of the workers.

Similar agreements were concluded in the other Nordic countries at the beginning of the 20th century, but do not exist in the other EC countries, where the trade unions have traditionally contested the managerial powers of employers.[1]

In the period from 1908 to 1910, the basic principles of conflict resolution through collective agreements were established. A fundamental distinction was drawn between conflicts of interest and conflicts of right. A conflict of interest arises in areas where no valid collective agreement applies. This may be because the matter in dispute has never been covered by

1 Compare C. SUMMERS, 'Comparisons in Labor Law: Sweden and the United States', in *Svensk Juristtidning*, 1983, p. 589 *et seq*.

a collective agreement, for example because the employer is not affiliated to an employers' organization; or it may be because a previously existing collective agreement has been terminated. In conflicts of interest the parties are free to take industrial action, including strike, lock-out, blacking and boycott.

A conflict of right arises where the matter in dispute is already covered by a collective agreement. A Danish collective agreement always includes a peace obligation, i.e. a duty on the parties to the collective agreement and their members not to take industrial action over a matter covered by the agreement. In the event of a conflict of right there is only in very few cases a right to resort to industrial action.

As an alternative to industrial action, a procedural system has been set up to enable aggrieved parties to obtain a judicial resolution of the conflict. This procedural system is sub-divided into two branches: industrial arbitration and the Labour Court (*Arbejdsretten*). In broad terms conflicts over the interpretation of collective agreements are settled by arbitration, whereas conflicts over an alleged breach of the collective agreement, such as strikes in violation of a peace obligation, are dealt with by the Labour Court, which can impose a fine (*bod*) on the workers or others who have violated the agreement. If the parties agree the case can be brought to industrial arbitration.

A standard grievance procedure for the handling of conflicts by industrial arbitration was laid down in a collective agreement in 1908 (*Normen for behandling af faglig strid*). Equal pay cases are in practice usually heard through industrial arbitration.

In collective labour law there is the above-mentioned special sanction, the *bod*, which is an amount of money the Labour Court can order a party to a collective agreement (or members of that party) to pay to the other party in the event of breach of the collective agreement.

The creation of the Welfare State 1930-1970

Most of the Danish Welfare State legislation dates back to the period from 1930 to around 1970. This includes legislation on unemployment and sickness benefits, holiday legislation, and legislation on maternity (and parental) leave. This kind of legislation provides for individual rights for employees.

The influence of EC law

To date, in line with the traditional Danish emphasis on collective agreements and labour market organizations, the main protection against abuse of the employer's discretionary authority has lain in the collective bargaining system and the grievance procedure concerning collective agreements. To a large extent employers still have the same managerial freedom as that recognized by the LO in the September Agreement of 1899. There is, for example, no general prohibition against unfair dismissals applying to all employment relationships, and there is no general employment Act in Denmark laying down minimum standards for terms and conditions in the individual employment relationship. For certain groups of employees such legislation does, however, exist. This is notably the case as regards salaried employees; the first Salaried Employees Act (*Funktionærloven*) was adopted in 1938.

A growing number of legal provisions do, however, limit the discretionary power of the employer by providing for worker participation in decisions regarding the working environment, unfair dismissals, introduction of new technology and sex equality, and by laying down statutory minimum standards on these subjects. The law on managerial prerogatives is being reformulated through this process.

EC law is inconsistent with basic features of the Danish labour law tradition, in that EC law provides stronger protection against discrimination as a fundamental individual (as opposed to collective) right and shows much less respect for collective agreements than is usual in the Danish tradition.

In the infringement case[1] brought against Denmark on equal pay the European Court of Justice (ECJ) ruled that Member States may leave the implementation of the principle of equal pay in the first instance to representatives of management and labour. That possibility does not, however, discharge them from the obligation of ensuring, by appropriate legislative and administrative provisions, that all workers are afforded the full protection provided for in the directive. That State guarantee must cover all cases where effective protection is not ensured by other means, for whatever reason.

A Danish collective agreement is only binding on an employer who, either individually or through membership of a participating employers' organization, is a party to the agreement. It is not binding on others and cannot be extended to cover outsiders. Danish collective agreements are therefore never sufficient as the sole instrument for implementing those EC directives which guarantee minimum rights for all workers. Denmark has to introduce legislation in traditional collective agreement areas when the EC adopts directives providing for minimum rights in these areas.

---

1 *Commission* v. *Denmark*, Case 143/83, [1985] ECR 427 (ECJ).

Gender and legal actors

In the Nordic countries, equality between the sexes has progressed to a certain extent, but not fully. It is the Scandinavian experience that the legal process and legal substance is influenced by gender matters and women's interests at an earlier stage than industrial relations procedures and practice. This is so in part because the collective bargaining process is male dominated.

EC law has met with a gender-related response among Danish labour law actors, probably due to the fact that the Danish labour law tradition is based on the most male-dominated bodies and EC law calls for a shift towards sources of law which in a Danish context are less male-dominated.

There is a comparatively high level of female representation in parliamentary bodies in the Nordic countries, of between 25 and 33 per cent, whereas women's share of decision-making bodies in labour market organizations is below 10 per cent.[1] This may account for some of the differences in the views on equality legislation between politicians, of whom about one-third are women, and representatives of the labour market organizations, who are predominantly male. Women also tend to gain influence on legal science and the judiciary (especially in the first instance courts) before winning an equal share of the decision-making positions in labour market organizations.

Politicians and legislators have been quite willing to use EC law as an argument for new legislation. Legal scholars have provided critical assessments of Danish law in the light of EC law and advocated a wider use of EC law and better compliance with it.

The Danish trade unions were unwilling to invoke EC law until the mid-1980s, even though they had been losing cases before the Danish courts involving the relevant EC law principles, such as the *Vejle Amts Folkeblad* and *Danfoss-I* cases.[2] At that point, a trade union with more than 80 per cent of women members (but very few women in decision-making positions) broke the abstentionist consensus and demanded a test of the compatibility of Danish legal practice with EC law before the ECJ. Following this change in attitude in one union (but not in the LO), questions concerning the burden of proof in equal pay cases[3] and the interpretation of equal

---

1 See on the difference between women's representation in the parliamentary and the corporate channels: *Det uferdige demokrati. Kvinner i nordisk politikk*, Oslo, 1983.

2 *Handels- og Kontorfunktionærernes Forbund i Danmark mod Dansk Arbejdsgiverforening/Danske Dagblades Forenings Forhandlingsorganisation for Vejle Amts Folkeblad*; and *Handels- og Kontorfunktionærernes Forbund i Danmark mod Dansk Arbejdsgiverforening for Danfoss A/S*; see Chapter 8 below.

3 *Handels- og Kontorfunktionærernes Forbund i Danmark* v. *Dansk Arbejdsgiverforening for Danfoss A/S*, Case 109/88, [1989] ECR 3199 (ECJ).

treatment[1] were referred to the ECJ for preliminary rulings under art. 177 of the EEC Treaty.

In Germany some judges in the first instance *Arbeitsgerichte* (labour courts), often women, have contributed to the integration of EC law on equality into national law by putting questions to the ECJ under art. 177(2) of the EEC Treaty.[2] The ECJ has shown a considerable willingness to deliver important judgments[3] in the field of labour law, not least in matters concerning women and equality. In Denmark, references have been submitted under art. 177(3) only.

1.1.2 ECONOMIC AND SOCIAL CONTEXT

Small and medium-sized enterprises

In the private sector in Denmark there are many small and medium-sized enterprises, and very few big enterprises. This has probably contributed to the policy trend of not wishing to put excessive burdens on employers in labour law.

High degree of unionization

The degree of union density in Denmark is around 80 to 90 per cent, both in the private and public sector, and both for unskilled and skilled workers, and for employees with different educational qualifications.

Large public sector

About one-third of the total workforce (about half of the female workforce) is employed in the public sector.

Many women in paid employment

In Denmark approximately the same number of men and women participate in the workforce.

---

1 *Handels- og Kontorfunktionærernes Forbund i Danmark for Birte Vibeke Hertz* v. *Dansk Arbejdsgiverforening for Aldi Marked K/S*, Case C-179/88, [1990] ECR I-3979 (ECJ).

2 See S. RAASCH, *Der Einfluß des Rechtes der Europäischen Gemeinschaften auf die Perspektiven der Richter im Arbeitsrecht zum Bereich Frauen und Arbeit in der Bundesrepublik Deutschland*, 1988 (unpublished research paper).

3 See H. RASMUSSEN, *On Law and Policy in the European Court of Justice*, Dordrecht, 1986.

The maintenance system [1]

In Europe men have not traditionally been provided for economically in the family, but have had to rely on a dual maintenance system based on income from employment (or independent occupations) and, if that failed, unemployment benefit, social security or social welfare, here called public maintenance.

The traditional maintenance system for women is in a process of dissolution and is gradually being replaced by the same dual maintenance system which applies to men. This transition for women provides a major socio-economic context for present-day equality legislation.

Denmark, Finland and Sweden are probably the Western countries in which this process has gone furthest but it seems to be happening in all EC Member States. Measured by the degree to which the transition to the dual maintenance system has been completed, Denmark is the most advanced EC country in equality matters. There are very few male sole breadwinners and very few dependent wives in Denmark. Discrimination problems stemming from gender-related maintenance systems are therefore rather old-fashioned from a Danish point of view. The most important equality problems in Denmark are related to gender segregation in the labour market which, in accordance with the Scandinavian experience generally, has not disappeared with the influx of women into employment.

Gender segregation in the labour market

There is a strong vertical gender segregation in Danish society. Women's share of leading positions is still very small. Women occupy only four per cent of top management posts in the private sector. Only two per cent of senior local authority managers are women, and women constitute only three per cent of senior managers in the State sector. Women's share is larger at middle management level; one in every ten middle managers is female in both the private and public sectors.

A lively debate has taken place in recent years concerning women's access to leading positions in Danish society within both politics and business. Prior to the adoption of the Act on Equality in Appointing Members to Public Committees etc., [2] which came into force in 1985, women comprised 12.7 per cent of State committee members. Women's share of new appointments increased to 38 per cent from 1985 to 1988.

---

1 See R. NIELSEN (ed.) *Women's Law in Scandinavia*, Copenhagen, 1982, p. 80.

2 Act No 157 of 24 April 1985.

There is also strong horizontal segregation; some sectors are male dominated and others are female dominated. This results in the coverage of collective agreements being gender related.[1]

1.2 SOURCES OF LAW

In labour law in general, the Danish tradition is that the Constitution and international law have been of very little importance and there are very few statutes. Instead, collective agreements, case law and unwritten principles of law constitute the main national sources of law. There is, however, a trend towards increased statutory regulation of the relationship between the employer and employees, mainly as a result of Denmark's membership of the EC.

Since the late 1970s, legislation has been the most important source of law in equality matters.

1.2.1 INTERNATIONAL STANDARDS

In matters of international law, Denmark has traditionally adhered to the dualistic theory. International conventions ratified by Denmark are not regarded as part of Danish law unless they are in some way incorporated into it. In labour law matters, especially as regards fundamental human rights, there are discrepancies between Danish law as it has traditionally been interpreted and international minimum standards. The dualistic theory has, however, been contested in recent years,[2] and it may now be possible to re-interpret Danish law so that it becomes compatible with international standards.

1.2.1.1 Human rights

Denmark has ratified a number of international conventions on human rights, but they have not been translated into national labour law and are usually not considered binding on public or private sector employers. It is, for example, the general view among Danish labour law experts that a private sector employer is free to make racist recruitment decisions.

The following conclusion concerning the Danish implementation of the European Social Charter of the Council of Europe may be mentioned as another example:[3]

---

1 See §2.3.2 below.

2 See O. ESPERSEN, *Indgåelse og opfyldelse af traktater,* Copenhagen, 1970, 163.

3 Per JACOBSEN in JASPERS and BETTEN (ed.), *25 years European Social Charter,* Kluwer, 1986, p. 81 *et seq*.

It is evident that the Danish governments have at no time had any intention of adhering strictly to those principles, if this would mean a necessity to abolish traditional principles of the Danish labour market. ... This means that the Charter cannot get a strong profile in the national state of law, and it must also necessarily mean that the national state of law on certain points may be in violation of the principles of the Charter.

1.2.1.2 Treaties on special questions

Denmark has ratified ILO Convention No 100 on Equal Remuneration (in 1960) and ILO Convention No 111 on Equal Treatment (in 1961), as well as the UN Convention of 1979 on the Elimination of All Forms of Discrimination against Women (in 1982). None of these conventions has been incorporated into Danish law by legislation.

Following the ratification of ILO Convention No 100 in 1960, the question whether or not to adopt legislation was raised in the Danish Parliament. The answer was in the negative[1] until in 1976 Denmark was obliged to adopt legislation on the issue in order to comply with Directive 75/117/EEC.

Denmark has a long-standing tradition of not providing special protection for women and has consequently not ratified such ILO conventions as that prohibiting night-work for women.[2]

1.2.2 EUROPEAN COMMUNITY LAW [3]

1.2.2.1 Direct effect of Community law

In its judgment of 8 April 1976 in the *Defrenne-II* case,[4] the ECJ held that art. 119 of the EEC Treaty has direct effect, but only within certain limits. It held that national courts have a duty to ensure the protection of the rights which art. 119 vests in individuals, in particular in relation to those forms of discrimination which have their origin in legislative provisions or collective labour agreements, as well as in cases where men and women receive unequal pay for equal work which is carried out in the same establishment or service, whether private or public.

The ECJ distinguished between direct and overt discrimination, which may be identified solely by means of the criteria laid down in art. 119 of the EEC Treaty, and more indirect and disguised forms of discrimination, which

---

1 For details see R. NIELSEN, *Kvindearbejdsret*, Copenhagen, 1979, p. 222.

2 See R. NIELSEN, 'Special protective legislation for women in the Nordic countries', *International Labour Review*, Vol. 119, No 1, Geneva, 1980.

3 See R. NIELSEN, 'The effect of Community law on the labour law of the Member States', Danish report for the 1988 FIDE Congress, printed in the Congress report, Vol. 2, pp 49-68.

4 *Defrenne* v. *Sabena* (No 2), Case 43/75, [1976] ECR 455 (ECJ).

can only be identified by means of more explicit implementing measures at Community or national level. The scope of the direct effect of art. 119 is confined to the relatively clear cases of direct discrimination, whereas the full implementation of the principle of equal opportunity embodied in art. 119 may necessitate the adoption of further appropriate measures. The distinction between direct and indirect discrimination is discussed in more detail below.

It had been the general opinion in Denmark until recently that Danish law on equality was sufficiently developed to cover at least the full substance of directly applicable EC provisions, so that there was no scope for Danish cases based directly on art. 119 of the EEC Treaty or the directives. Since the ruling of the ECJ in the *Rinner-Kühn* case,[1] it has been argued[2] that s. 5 of the Salaried Employees Act, which limits the entitlement to sick pay to employees who work a minimum of 15 hours work per week, violates art. 119 of the EEC Treaty as interpreted in *Rinner-Kühn*. A Danish female salaried employee who works less than 15 hours per week should therefore be able to claim pay during periods of sickness before a Danish court under art. 119 of the EEC Treaty.

It follows from the judgment in *Marshall* v. *Southampton and South-West Hampshire Area Health Authority*[3] that Directive 76/207/EEC has no direct effect in relation to private sector employers. Some of its provisions, such as art. 5, are directly effective against a public employer. It is the prevailing opinion in Denmark that it also follows from the *Marshall* case that Directive 75/117/EEC has no direct effect against private sector employers.[4] The ECJ has held in some cases[5] that art. 4 of Directive 79/7/EEC is directly effective.

The Labour Market Supplementary Pensions Act and the Unemployment Benefits Act, which only accord limited rights to part-time workers, are probably in contravention of art. 4 of Directive 79/7/EEC as interpreted in the *Ruzius-Wilbrink* case.[6]

1 *Rinner-Kühn* v. *FWW Spezial-Gebäudereinigung GmbH & Co KG*, Case 171/88, [1989] ECR 2743 (ECJ).

2 See R. NIELSEN, *Judiciel aktivisme i EF-arbejdsretten*, Retfærd, 1979.

3 Case 152/84, [1986] ECR 723 (ECJ).

4 See GULMANN and HAGEL-SØRENSEN, *EF-ret*, Copenhagen, 1989.

5 See e.g. *Borrie Clarke* v. *Chief Adjudication Officer*, Case 384/85, [1987] ECR 2865 (ECJ); *Ruzius-Wilbrink* v. *Bestuur van de Bedrijfsvereniging voor Overheidsdiensten*, Case C-102/88, [1989] ECR 4311 (ECJ).

6 See previous footnote.

1.2.2.2 Retrospective implementation

In the *Defrenne-II* case, the ECJ ruled that neither the Resolution of the Member States of 30 December 1961 nor Directive 75/117/EEC were capable of validly postponing the date on which the equal pay principle became effective. But the Court drew a distinction between the 'theoretical' date for implementing the equal pay principle (i.e. 1 January 1962 in the original Member States and 1 January 1973 in Denmark, Ireland and the United Kingdom), and the date from which its direct effect could be invoked; it held that the direct effect of art. 119 of the EEC Treaty could not be relied on to support claims concerning pay periods prior to the date of the judgment (i.e. 8 April 1976), except as regards those workers who had already brought legal proceedings or made an equivalent claim.

In Denmark equal pay rates in collective agreements between the LO and DA were introduced as of 1 April 1973, three months after the beginning of direct effect for art. 119 of the EEC Treaty, but there were no claims based directly on art. 119.

1.2.3 CONSTITUTIONAL LAW AND SOCIAL RIGHTS

The Danish Constitution contains no provision relating to equality between men and women and only a few provisions of relevance to the labour market.[1] There is, for example, no ban on discrimination on grounds of sex, race or ethnic origin in the Constitution; and there is no constitutional protection of the right to strike. There is, however, some protection of freedom of association.

1.2.4 LEGISLATION

1.2.4.1 Prior legislation

In most European countries, legislation providing for some sort of equal access to public positions was introduced in the period shortly after women won the right to vote in general elections. In Norway women were enfranchised in 1907 and an Act on Equal Access to the Public Sector was enacted in 1912. In Denmark the corresponding years were 1915 and 1921; in the United Kingdom (then including Ireland), 1918 and 1919; in Germany (the Weimar Republic), 1919 and 1919; in Sweden, 1921 and 1923. In the other EC Member States this development occurred in the period around, or after, the Second World War: in France, for example, in 1944 and 1945.

---

1 See D. ZISKIND, *Labor Provisions in Constitutions of Europe: Comparative Labor Law,* 1984, p. 311.

Apart from the above-mentioned 1921 Act (the Act on Equal Access to Public Positions[1]), there was practically no legislation on equality in Denmark before the implementation of the EC directives on the subject in the late 1970s.

In recruitment in the private sector, both direct and indirect sex discrimination were considered lawful until the implementation of Directive 76/207/EEC by the Equal Treatment Act of 1978. It was also lawful for a private employer to dismiss on grounds of pregnancy.

Equal pay has for many years been a traditional collective labour law issue in Denmark, which was settled by the social partners by collective bargaining without statutory intervention.

The question as to whether or not to adopt legislation on equal pay was raised in Denmark before entry into the Community as of 1 January 1973. A big majority in Parliament rejected proposals for equal pay legislation in the late 1960s and early 1970s.[2] The main argument was that the collective autonomy of the labour market parties should be respected and the issue left to regulation by collective agreement. Denmark's membership of the EC changed this view.

In his article 'On Uses and Misuses of Comparative Law', Otto Kahn-Freund argued that the link between law and the political power structures today constitutes the main impediment to the transplant of law from one country to another. Applied to labour law, this means that collective labour law, which cannot really be altered without upsetting the balance of power between the 'social partners' (trade unions and employers' organizations), is more difficult to transfer from country to country than individual employment law; and that rules on institutions and procedures are more closely tied to the national context than substantive rules. In cases where the Constitution codifies the political history of a country, this too is relatively hard to transplant.[3]

A comparison of the changes implemented in Denmark, compared with the law of the other Nordic States not in the EC, illustrates Kahn-Freund's thesis on the transferability of law and the traditional Nordic perspective on the relative role of legislation and collective agreements on equal pay. Denmark has given up its resistance to equal pay legislation. On the other hand in Sweden there is no statutory guarantee of equal pay for work of equal value unless the labour market organizations have agreed in a

---

1 *Lov nr. 100 af 1921 om lige adgang for kvinder og mænd til tjenestestillinger og hverv*, Act No 100 of 1921.

2 See for more details R. NIELSEN, *Kvindearbejdsret*, Copenhagen, 1979.

3 O. KAHN-FREUND, 'On Uses and Misuses of Comparative Law', in O. KAHN-FREUND, *Selected Writings*, London, 1978, pp 294-319.

collective agreement that the work in question is of equal value. The Swedish provisions on equal pay were partly inspired by the British Equal Pay Act 1970 as it was before being amended in consequence of the ruling of the ECJ against the United Kingdom.[1]

The difference between developments in Denmark, which has given up its traditional adherence to collective self-regulation in equal pay matters, and those in Sweden, which has retained it with regard to equal value problems, may support the thesis that the influence of EC law is able to overcome the traditional nature of collective labour law and thereby make the distinction suggested by Kahn-Freund between the transferability of individual and collective labour law less relevant. The fact that equal pay to some degree has remained a subject for the labour market organizations to decide by collective agreement in Sweden and that national differences have survived is a sign of the special importance the organizations attach to equal pay compared to other equality matters and partly confirms Kahn-Freund's thesis.

The development of the Single European Market has, however, inspired Sweden to reconsider its equality legislation in the light of EC law. An amendment to the Swedish Equality Act is under preparation. As part of the preparatory work the Swedish Equality Ombudsman in 1989 commissioned a report on the Swedish Act from a European perspective[2] in which the discrepancies between Swedish law and EC law are highlighted. It is a possibility that Sweden may choose to adapt to EC law even though it is not a Member State of the Community.

1.2.4.2 Present legislation

A statute on equal pay was adopted in 1976[3] to implement Directive 75/117/EEC. Originally the wording of the Act did not mention work of equal value. The Commission took proceedings against Denmark on this ground, claiming that Denmark had failed to comply with the directive. The ECJ found against Denmark.[4] The Act was then amended in 1986, and a new amendment to the Equal Pay Act was introduced in 1989,[5] which gave the Equal Status Council (*Ligestillingsrådet*) the power to demand disclosure of information from employers in equal pay cases. In 1992 the Equal Pay Act was again amended, adapting the text of the Act to developments which had taken place in case law; this Consolidation Act is the legislation currently in

---

1 *Commission* v. *United Kingdom*, Case 61/81, [1982] ECR 2601 (ECJ).

2 R. NIELSEN, *Den svenska jämställdhetslagstiftningen i europeiskt perspektiv*, Copenhagen, 1989.

3 *Lov nr. 32 af 1976 med senere ændringer om lige løn til mænd og kvinder*, Act No 32 of 4 February 1976, as amended by Act No 65 of 19 February 1986.

4 Case 143/83.

5 Act No 244 of 1989.

force in relation to equal pay, and is hereafter referred to as the Equal Pay Act.[1]

The Equal Treatment Act[2] was enacted in 1978 in order to implement Directive 76/207/EEC. The Act was amended in 1984 to persuade the Commission of the European Communities to drop infringement proceedings brought against Denmark. Further amendments were adopted in 1989.[3]

A new Act in 1989 on Equal Treatment and Parental Leave[4] brought together the former Equal Treatment Act and the Parental Leave Act[5] into one Act. The relevant law is now to be found in a Consolidation Act of 1990, hereafter referred to as the Equal Treatment Act.[6] It contains the following provisions:

- the granting of powers to the Equal Status Council to grant positive action exemptions;[7]
- the raising of the maximum level of compensation for dismissal of an employee who asserts her right from 26 weeks' pay to 39 weeks' pay,[8] provision for reinstatement in cases of dismissal on grounds of pregnancy or parental leave,[9] and compensation for dismissal on grounds of pregnancy or parental leave of 78 weeks' wages;[10]
- an explicit provision in the text of the Act implementing a reversal of the burden of proof and reinstatement in cases of unlawful dismissal during pregnancy or parental leave;[11] and

---

1 *Lovbekendtgørelse nr. 639 af 1992 af lov om lige løn til mænd og kvinder*, Consolidation Act No 639 of 1992 on Equal Pay for Men and Women.

2 *Lov nr. 161 af 1978 med senere ændringer om ligebehandling af mænd og kvinder med hensyn til beskæftigelse med videre*, Act No 161 of 1978 on Equal Treatment, as amended by Act No 117 of 1984.

3 Act No 244 of 1989.

4 *Lov nr. 244 af 1989 med senere ændringer om ligebehandling af mænd og kvinder med hensyn til beskæftigelse og barselsorlov*, Act No 244 of 1989 on Equal Treatment between Men and Women as regards Employment, Parental Leave etc.

5 *Lov nr. 234 af 1980 med senere ændringer om barselsorlov*, Act No 234 of 1980.

6 *Lovbekendtgørelse nr. 686 af 1990 om ligebehandling af mænd og kvinder med hensyn til beskæftigelse og barselsorlov m.v.*, Consolidation Act No 686 of 1990 on Equal Treatment for Men and Women in Employment, Parental Leave etc.

7 Section 13 (2)-(4) of the Act.

8 Section 15(2).

9 Section 16(1).

10 Section 16(2) and (3).

11 Section 16(4).

- the duty on the part of employers and employees to give information to the Equal Status Council in discrimination cases; there is a criminal sanction (in the form of a fine) for violation of this obligation.[1]

The Equal Pay Act as amended imposes a similar duty on employers and employees to give information to the Equal Status Council in equal pay cases. In accordance with s. 5a of that Act there is a criminal sanction (a fine) for violation of this obligation.

The Equal Status Council was established administratively by the Prime Minister in 1975 on the recommendation of the Commission on the Status of Women in Society (*Kvindekommissionen*). The Council was confirmed by law on 12 April 1978, on the same date as the Equal Treatment Act was passed. The latter Act provides for equal treatment between men and women as regards access to employment and related matters. The Equal Opportunities Act[2] has now replaced a previous Act on the Equal Status Council.

In 1985 an Act on Equality in Appointing Members to Public Committees etc. was passed. It was replaced in 1990 by the present Act.

---

1 Section 18.

2 *Lov nr. 238 af 1988 med senere ændringer om ligestilling mellem mænd og kvinder*, Act No 238 of 1988.

2. BASIC CONCEPTS

2.1 EQUALITY AND DISCRIMINATION

The significant changes in the social context of gender issues which have been occurring during the last 20 years form the general background to the framework of equality laws. Social and technological developments have rendered gender-related qualifications obsolete and created a demand for new qualifications and more mobility across gender-related boundaries in the labour market.

In the Scandinavian debate[1] on how to conceptualize sex discrimination and equality, a distinction has been drawn between three different but inter-connected meanings of gender or sex:

- a dichotomous, biological concept of sex according to which there are two sexes: women and men;
- a multi-variable, biological concept according to which persons are regarded as qualified by their sex when they are in biologically sex-related circumstances, e.g. women of fertile age as opposed to women of non-fertile age, pregnant women as opposed to women who are not pregnant etc.;
- a social gender concept where the consequences of social conditions, which in a given historical context are typical for women or men (for example, that many women combine family work and employment-related work, do part-time work, are employed in typical women's jobs in a sex-segregated labour market etc.), are regarded as gender-related.

The assessment of sex discrimination differs according to which of these sex or gender concepts one applies.

The dichotomous, biological concept of sex corresponds to a notion of sex discrimination which is understood as the different treatment of men and women in comparable circumstances. Problems regarding sex discrimination between women and women do not arise in this conceptual context.

The multi-variable, biological gender concept implies that sex discrimination can take place between women and women (e.g. when an employer selects a woman of non-fertile age rather than a woman of fertile age, a non-pregnant woman rather than a pregnant woman, a childless woman rather than a mother of a small child etc.) and does not require a comparison between women and men. Because of the gender segregation of the labour market, sex-based discrimination between women is probably as

---

1 R. NIELSEN, *Equality Legislation in a Comparative Perspective — Towards State Feminism?*, Copenhagen, 1983.

widespread in Denmark as sex-based discrimination between men and women.

The social gender concept corresponds to an understanding of sex discrimination linked to the social functioning of the law in a given context. A prohibition based on this concept renders it unlawful to operate practices which under the given circumstances result in inequalities between the sexes, regardless of whether the discriminator intended these inequalities or in any way actively worked for them. This concept of gender shifts the focus from the (hidden or overtly admitted) motive of the discriminator to the objective outcome of his acts in the particular context.

2.2 DIRECT DISCRIMINATION

2.2.1 DEFINITION

The prohibition of discrimination implies that each applicant is individually entitled to equal treatment. According to the explanatory remarks attached to the Equal Treatment Act,[1] it is a basic principle that each individual must be considered on his or her own merit regardless of sex.

2.2.1.1 Reason

If the employer's decision is connected with the sex of the employee there is direct discrimination, regardless of whether the employer openly admits the motive or tries to hide it. It is direct discrimination, in breach of the Equal Treatment Act, where the employer refuses to select an applicant on grounds of sex and subsequently employs a better-qualified applicant of the opposite sex. In this case the result could have been achieved legally by preferring the best qualified applicant on grounds of qualifications, but if the employer's motive was discriminatory (and this can be proved), then it is a violation of the law.

2.2.1.2 Detriment

It is not a condition under Danish law that different treatment on grounds of sex needs to be to the detriment of anyone in order for the employer to have committed unlawful sex discrimination. If for example an employer gives Christmas gifts to the employees and differentiates by sex, this will probably be unlawful even when the value of the gifts chosen for the men and women is the same.

---

1 *Folketingstidende* 1977-1978, appendix A, p. 3087.

2.2.1.3 Comparator

In case of sex discrimination based on the multi-variable, biological gender concept or the social gender concept, there is no need for an individual woman to find an individual male comparator.

The selection of pregnant women rather than non-pregnant women for dismissal is an example of a violation of s. 5 of the Danish Equal Treatment Act. There is case law[1] to support this interpretation.

2.2.2 EXTENDED DEFINITION

According to s. 1 of the Equal Treatment Act the prohibition of sex discrimination applies to indirect as well as to direct discrimination. As examples of indirect discrimination the Act makes reference to pregnancy, marriage or family position. Section 1 corresponds to art. 2(1) of Directive 76/207/EEC which, however, does not mention pregnancy.

2.2.2.1 Marital and family status

Discrimination on grounds of marital status is expressly given as an example of indirect discrimination in s. 1 of the Equal Treatment Act. The same applies to discrimination on grounds of family status and pregnancy.

2.2.2.2 Sexual harassment

Sexual harassment is a violation of the Equal Treatment Act. This view has been taken in Danish legal literature since the mid-1980s.[2]

This interpretation has now clearly also been accepted in case law.[3] In one case,[4] a woman was awarded DKR 40,000 (approximately ECU 5,000) from her employer as compensation for sexual harassment under ss 4 and 8 of the Equal Treatment Act. In another case,[5] a sexually harassed woman was awarded DKR 100,000 (approximately ECU 12,500) from her employer for his violation of s. 4 of the Equal Treatment Act and s. 3 of the Salaried Employees Act.[6]

---

1 See U 1981, 729.

2 See in particular A. ANDERSEN and R. NIELSEN, *Ligestillingslovene med kommentarer*, 1st edition, Copenhagen, 1986; 2nd edition, Copenhagen, 1990, and H. PETERSEN, 'Retsbeskyttelse af kvinders værdighed', *TFR*, 1988, p. 253.

3 See in particular U 1990, 92, and U 1992, 18.

4 U 1990, 92.

5 U 1992, 18.

6 *Lov nr. 261 af 1948 med senere ændringer om retsforholdet mellem arbejdsgivere og funktionærer*, Act No 261 of 1948.

In a recent criminal case,[1] a male employee who had committed serious sexual harassment received a suspended prison sentence of six months for violation of s. 220 of the Criminal Code[2] and was sentenced to pay DKR 20,000 as compensation under s. 26 of the Damages Act.[3] The Equal Treatment Act, which imposes obligations on employers, was not considered applicable in a case taken against an employee. A case is now being brought against the employer for violation of the Equal Treatment Act.

All the above cases deal with sexual harassment consisting of some sort of verbal or physical activity directed towards individual victims.

In one much debated case a major employer used a picture of a half-naked blonde woman as an illustration for safety instructions in the workplace. Female employees at the workplace complained anonymously to the Equal Status Council that this constituted sexual harassment in violation of the Equal Treatment Act. In the debate it has been argued that use of women as eye-catchers is a violation of s. 4 of the Equal Treatment Act and is in contravention of the Council Resolution of May 1990 on the Protection of Women's Dignity at Work for which the Danish Government has expressed support.

2.2.2.3 Physical attributes

It is direct discrimination in violation of the Equal Treatment Act if both men and women are employed in a job category but are selected by means of different criteria: for example, where women are chosen because of their looks, charm and social qualifications, while men are chosen on grounds of professional criteria.

2.3 INDIRECT DISCRIMINATION

2.3.1 DEFINITION

Indirect discrimination is related to the social gender concept. In a case of indirect discrimination the employer's motive is irrelevant. What matters is whether the criteria he used in the particular social conditions have a gender-related effect. The prohibition of indirect discrimination does not mean that it is forbidden to use criteria with such an effect, but that the employer must be able to give objective reasons for using them.

---

1 Decided on 17 January 1992, unreported.

2 *Borgerlig Straffelov af 15. april 1930.*

3 *Lov nr. 228 af 1984 med senere ændringer om erstatningsansvar,* Act No 228 of 1984.

2.3.2 SUSPECT CRITERIA

Part-time work

The part-time criterion is widely used in Danish legislation. In the light of the ECJ decisions in *Rinner-Kühn*[1] and *Ruzius-Wilbrink*,[2] it is possible to question the compatibility with EC law of a number of Danish laws, in particular the Salaried Employees Act (in relation to sick pay), the Unemployment Benefits Act[3] and the Labour Market Supplementary Pensions Act.[4]

In *Jenkins* v. *Kingsgate (Clothing Productions) Ltd*,[5] the ECJ was presented with the problem of whether different hourly rates for full-time and part-time workers constituted a breach of EC law provisions on equal pay. The ECJ did not hold that discrimination between part-time and full-time workers constitutes indirect discrimination on grounds of sex *per se*; it declared a difference in pay between part-time and full-time workers to be a breach of art. 119 of the EEC Treaty only if it is in reality an indirect way of reducing women's pay (because most part-time workers are women). Whether this is the case in fact is a matter for the national courts.

In *Bilka-Kaufhaus GmbH* v. *Weber von Hartz*,[6] the ECJ considered whether access to an occupational pension scheme which excluded part-time workers could be seen as 'pay' within the meaning of art. 119 of the EEC Treaty. The ECJ noted that according to the documents before the Court the occupational pension scheme at issue in the main proceedings, although adopted in accordance with the provisions laid down by German legislation for such schemes, was based on an agreement between *Bilka* and the staff committee representing its employees and had the effect of supplementing the social benefits paid under national legislation of general application with benefits financed entirely by the employer.

The ECJ found that if a much lower proportion of women than of men worked full-time, the exclusion of part-time workers from the occupational pension scheme would be contrary to art. 119 of the EEC Treaty where, taking into account the difficulties encountered by women workers in working full-time, that measure could not be justified by factors which excluded any discrimination on grounds of sex. However, if the undertaking

---

1 Case 171/88, [1989] ECR 2743 (ECJ).

2 Case C-102/88, [1989] ECR 4311 (ECJ).

3 *Lov nr. 114 af 1970 med senere ændringer om arbejdsløshedsforsikring og arbejdsformidling*, Act No 114 of 1970.

4 *Lov nr. 46 af 1964 med senere ændringer om arbejdsmarkedets tillægspension*, Act No 46 of 1964.

5 Case 96/80, [1981] ECR 911 (ECJ).

6 Case 170/84, [1986] ECR 1607 (ECJ).

were able to show that its pay practice could be objectively justified on grounds unrelated to any discrimination on grounds of sex, there was no breach of art. 119.

It has been argued in Danish legal literature[1] that it follows from the *Bilka* case that Danish case law, as found in the *Vejle Amts Folkeblad* case and the *Danpo* case,[2] is inconsistent with EC law.

In *Rinner-Kühn* the ECJ ruled that a statutory provision excluding employees working no more than ten hours work per week from sick pay is contrary to art. 119 of the EEC Treaty if it results in a far greater number of women than men being excluded, unless the Member State shows that the exclusion is based on objectively justified factors unrelated to any discrimination on grounds of sex.

In the light of this judgment, it has been argued[3] in Danish legal literature that s. 5 of the Salaried Employees Act (on sick pay), which excludes employees with less than 15 hours work per week, and possibly a number of other Danish statutory provisions using the part-time criterion, are inconsistent with art. 119 of the EEC Treaty. The *Ruzius-Wilbrink* decision may also be relied upon to contest the compatibility with Directive 79/7/EEC of the Unemployment Benefits Act and the Labour Market Supplementary Pensions Act.

The Danish case law relating to the part-time criterion has in general concerned situations where men were denied part-time jobs, in situations where such jobs were open to women (see §4.7.6 below).

Marital status, family status, pregnancy, breadwinner

Discrimination on grounds of marital or family status is probably not widespread in Denmark. However, the dismissal of pregnant women has been at issue in many of the Danish dismissal cases in which sex discrimination was alleged.[4]

An example of indirect sex discrimination with reference to marital status was contained in a case of 18 February 1975 before the Labour Court.[5] An employer made four unmarried men redundant at a male-dominated workplace. The Labour Court considered marital status a reasonable

---

1 R. NIELSEN and K. PRECHT, *EF-regler om ligeløn — perspektiver for dansk ret*, U 1988, B 169.

2 See Chapter 8.

3 R. NIELSEN, 'Judiciel aktivisme i EF-arbejdsretten — en ny dom om diskrimination af ansatte med kort deltid', *Retfærd*, No 47, Copenhagen, 1989.

4 See Chapter 8.

5 Case No 7400.

criterion, which should not however be the sole factor. Today such a dismissal would be in contravention of s. 4 of the Equal Treatment Act. The former practice is illustrated in a ruling of 26 October 1933.[1] The municipality of Århus had dismissed six married women who were selected for dismissal because they were married, and this was held to be lawful. Act No 100 of 1921 was not taken into consideration.[2] Such a case would today be in obvious contravention of Act No 100 of 1921 and of the Equal Treatment Act.

Mobility requirement

There is no Danish material on the lawfulness of a mobility requirement. It can perhaps be inferred from the ECJ decision in *Danfoss*[3] that such requirements are lawful in the same circumstances as are flexibility requirements.

Strength

The prohibition against discrimination implies that each applicant is entitled to individual treatment. According to the explanatory remarks attached to the Equal Treatment Act,[4] it is a basic principle that each individual must be considered on his or her own merits regardless of sex. It would therefore be a violation of the law if, for example, men were preferred for a job which required physical strength because men on average are stronger than women.

In *Rummler* v. *Dato-Druck GmbH*,[5] the ECJ found that any criterion based on values appropriate only to workers of one sex carries with it a risk of discrimination and may jeopardize the main objective of the directive. Directive 75/117/EEC does not prohibit the use, in a job classification system used for the purpose of determining rates of pay, of the criterion of the need for muscular effort or that of the heaviness of the work if, in view of the nature of the tasks involved, the work to be performed requires the use of a certain degree of physical strength, so long as the system as a whole, by taking into account other criteria, precludes any discrimination on grounds of sex.

---

1 Case No 1846.

2 See O. KRARUP and J. MATTHIASSEN, *Afskedigelsesret,* Copenhagen, 1984, p. 127.

3 *Handels- og Kontorfunktionærernes Forbund i Danmark v. Dansk Arbejdsgiverforening for Danfoss,* Case 109/88, [1989] ECR 3199 (ECJ).

4 *Folketingstidende* 1977-78, appendix A, p. 3087.

5 Case 237/85, [1986] ECR 2101 (ECJ).

Age limits

In the United Kingdom the imposition of an upper age limit of 28 years for appointment in the public sector has been found to be indirect discrimination; because of family obligations women have a greater need than men to have the opportunity to start their careers late. In the Danish social context it is unusual for women to leave the labour market when having small children. This criterion does not necessarily therefore raise the same suspicions of indirect discrimination in Denmark.

Minimum height

In the Danish police force different height requirements apply for men and women.

Preferences for existing employees

There is no Danish material examining the lawfulness of internal vocational training, or selection for promotion among existing employees, which are widespread practices both in male and female-dominated workplaces.

Collective agreements

A number of suspect criteria are involved in the operation of collective agreements. Different wage systems are used in Denmark. In the normal wage system workers receive the rates laid down in the collective agreement and nothing more. In the minimum wage system, the collective agreement lays down the minimum wage. Most workers or employees receive increments based on a very wide variety of criteria. It is difficult to know to what extent the criteria for receiving increments within the minimum wage system are indirectly discriminatory. Danish case law deals in particular with the following suspect criteria: seniority, vocational training and flexibility. The fact that the same work is covered by different collective agreements for men and women may also give rise to discrimination.

Seniority

The lawfulness of pay increases based on seniority was dealt with by the ECJ in *Danfoss*. The company applied a collective agreement within the minimum wage system which set basic rates of pay for the various grades of workers, but allowed for individual increments based on flexibility, vocational training and seniority. The ECJ found that where an undertaking applies a pay system which is characterized by a total lack of transparency, the burden of proof is on the employer to show that his wage practice is not discriminatory where a female worker establishes, by comparison with a relatively large number of employees, that the average pay of female workers is lower than that of male workers. The ECJ accepted that an employer can justify pay differences between men and women by reference to seniority without having to show that seniority is particularly relevant. This view was modified in *Nimz* v. *Freie und Hansestadt Hamburg*.[1]

In Denmark, the arbitrator in an industrial arbitration tribunal delivered his verdict on 13 November 1992 in an equal pay case between the Salaried Employees' Union (HK) and the employers' organization in the dairy sector (acting on behalf of Frisko Sol, which is a subsidiary of the Danish Unilever Limited, which is in turn a subsidiary of the multinational Unilever Group). The case was about a man and a woman who performed work of equal value but received different pay. Initially the employer did not contest the claim that the two employees did work of equal value, but claimed that the difference in pay was due to a considerable difference in seniority. At the final hearing the employer argued in addition that the work in question was of different value. The arbitrator found partly in favour of HK: it was accepted that the work performed was of different value for a period. In the period when that was not the case (i.e. when the work was of equal value), the difference in seniority was rejected as insufficient to justify unequal pay. During the oral hearing it was argued by HK that it followed from *Nimz* that seniority was not by itself a sufficient justification for different remuneration.

It had been customary, until this arbitration award, not to award interest when a case was brought before an industrial arbitration tribunal. In this case HK claimed interest from the date on which proceedings had been initiated. The employer protested, invoking the previous Danish custom. In support of HK's view it was argued that it followed from the underlying EC provisions that interest should be awarded, and that judgment in the *Marshall-II* case, then pending before the ECJ, would have to be awaited if the arbitrator thought otherwise. The arbitrator decided the case immediately, but reinterpreted Danish law by disregarding the Danish custom of not awarding interest, and found that it followed from the Interest on Overdue Payments Act[2] that the employer had to pay interest.

In the Danish context this award is interesting mainly for two reasons. First, it made it clear that a difference in seniority is not by itself a sufficient justification for unequal pay. Secondly, it changed the Danish practice on the awarding of interest in cases before industrial arbitration tribunals. In that respect the Danish decision went further than what was required by EC law, in that the arbitrator put an interpretation on the Interest on Overdue Payments Act which will apply in all cases before industrial arbitration tribunals, and not only in cases where EC law is at issue. It thus provides an example of interpretation of national law in conformity with EC law where

---

1 Case C-184/89, [1991] ECR I-297 (ECJ).

2 *Lov nr. 638 af 1977 med senere ændringer om renter ved forsinket betaling*, Act No 638 of 1977.

the problem of creating consistency between national law and EC law is resolved by raising the standard of national law to such a high level that it is unnecessary to wait for the judgment of the ECJ in *Marshall-II* or to ask questions concerning the duty under EC law to pay interest.

Vocational training

In a case concerning *Vejle Amts Folkeblad* (a local newspaper), the question was whether male skilled typographers and female skilled clerical workers doing the same work (typing advertisements), who were covered by two different collective agreements (one for graphic workers and another for clerical workers), should receive equal pay. The graphic workers' agreement provided for better pay (irrespective of the sex of the graphic worker) than that provided for in the clerical workers' agreement (equally irrespective of the sex of the clerical worker). In Denmark most graphic workers are men and most clerical workers are women. The arbitration award[1] of February 1985 was in favour of the employer. It stated that in cases involving skilled workers differences in vocational training can justify different pay.

Vocational training as a pay criterion was at issue in *Danfoss*. The ECJ held that an employer could justify pay differences by reference to vocational training if, and only if, that training is relevant to the work actually performed. Following the judgment of the ECJ in *Danfoss*, the *Vejle Amts Folkeblad* award can no longer be considered an accurate expression of current law, since the difference in vocational training was of no relevance to the work actually performed at *Vejle Amts Folkeblad*.

Until the judgment of the ECJ in *Danfoss*, the full burden of proof was on the employee. In an arbitration award of April 1985[2] it was held that the employees had not proved that the wage difference could not be due to reasons other than sex. Consequently the arbitrator found in favour of the employer. The burden of proof placed upon the employees in this case is in practice impossible to discharge.

Flexibility

In the *Danfoss* case, flexibility was determined by an overall assessment of the quality of work, taking into account the amount of work done by an employee and the employee's enthusiasm and sense of initiative. Employees did not know how these criteria were applied and were therefore unable to compare the various elements of their pay. However, the average pay of male

1 Arbitration award of 11 February 1985, published in *Arbejdsretligt Tidsskrift,* 1985, p. 185.

2 Arbitration award of 16 April 1985 in the *Danfoss-I* case, published in *Arbejdsretligt Tidsskrift*, 1985, p. 197.

workers was 6.85 per cent higher than that of female workers in the same category.

The ECJ held that where pay is based on an assessment of the quality of work, and this results in systematic unfairness to female workers, this can only be because the employer has applied it in an abusive manner. It is inconceivable that the work carried out by female workers would be generally of a lower quality. The employer may not therefore justify the use of such a criterion where its application shows itself to be systematically unfair to women.

Different collective agreements

The structure of the Danish labour market is such that female-dominated groups are often covered by different collective agreements than those applying to groups made up largely of men.

With technological development the groups consisting mainly of women and those consisting of men to an increasing extent carry out the same jobs. Denmark has a women-only trade union (*Kvindeligt Arbejderforbund i Danmark — KAD*) for various categories of unskilled women workers. Unskilled male workers doing the same work (or work of equal value) will be members of another, male-dominated, union, the *Specialarbejderforbundet i Danmark* (SiD). In some cases the two unions have concluded joint collective agreements; in other cases they are parties to separate collective agreements. These parallel agreements covering the same work (or work of equal value) do not always provide for the same pay; sometimes the male agreement provides for extra pay in situations where the woman's agreement does not. In these situations women and men doing the same work (or work of equal value) will receive different remuneration. This is a violation of the equal pay principle both under EC law and under Danish law as it is interpreted in judicial practice.

There are two arbitration awards, one from 1977[1] and another from 1987,[2] in which it was held that unskilled male and female workers doing the same work or work of equal value must be paid equal pay. The fact that they are covered by two different collective agreements cannot be used as an excuse for different pay for women and men.

There are, however, still some problems relating to different collective agreements. The judgment of the Danish Supreme Court in the *Danpo* case[3] illustrates this (see §4.8.2 below).

1 Arbitration award of 8 December 1977 in the *FDB* case.

2 Arbitration award of 29 April 1987 in the *Premier Is* case.

3 U 1983, 379.

It is also sometimes found that a women's agreement allows part-time work while the men's agreement prohibits it, resulting in men being barred from part-time work in situations where it is open to women (see §4.7.6 below).

2.3.3 DISPROPORTIONATE IMPACT

Statistical evidence

In the *Danfoss* case the ECJ ruled that where an undertaking applies a pay system which is characterized by a total lack of transparency, the burden of proof is on the employer to show that his wage practice is not discriminatory where a female worker establishes, by comparison with a relatively large number of employees, that the average pay of female workers is lower than that of male workers. Sophisticated statistical calculations are thus unnecessary to shift the burden of proof. A calculation of average pay is sufficient.

Relevant pools

In the *Danfoss* case, the ECJ was asked whether an employee, by establishing that an employer who employs a large number (for example at least 100) on average pays women less than men, can show that Directive 75/117/EEC has been violated. The court confined itself to requiring a comparison between a relatively large number of employees. In a Danish context, with many small and medium-sized employers and only few employers with more than 100 employees (Danfoss is one of Denmark's largest employers), this is interpreted as meaning that differences in average pay can also be used to shift the burden of proof at smaller enterprises.[1] The persons being compared must do work of equal value.

Impact on the individual

Where a trade union contests the lawfulness of a pay practice or the validity of a collective agreement and seeks a declaratory judgment, there is no need for an individual victim. The previously mentioned *Danpo* case[2] was brought by the Women Workers' Union, which sought a declaratory judgment that its own collective agreement was partly invalid.

---

1 R. NIELSEN and K. PRECHT, *Procesret og ligeløn — nye EF-krav til dansk ret*, Copenhagen, 1990.

2 U 1983, 379.

2.3.4 OBJECTIVE JUSTIFICATION

In the *Bilka* case,[1] the ECJ held that under art. 119 of the EEC Treaty a department store may justify the adoption of a pay policy excluding part-time workers from its occupational pension scheme on the ground that it seeks to employ as few part-time workers as possible, where it is found that the means chosen for achieving that objective correspond to a real need on the part of the undertaking, are appropriate with a view to achieving the objective in question and are necessary to that end.

In the *Danfoss* case questions were asked regarding the defences an employer can use to discharge the burden of proof. The employer can only justify pay differences by reference to vocational training or flexibility if that training or flexibility is relevant to the work as actually performed. The employer can justify pay differences by reference to seniority without having to show why seniority is relevant.

It follows from Danish case law (see the two arbitration awards from 1977[2] and 1987[3] mentioned above) that the existence of different collective agreements is not a legitimate defence.

2.4 VICTIMIZATION

Victimization is explicitly prohibited both by the Equal Pay Act and the Equal Treatment Act. By virtue of the amendment to the Equal Treatment Act in 1989 the maximum level of compensation for dismissal of an employee who asserts her right was raised from 26 weeks' pay to 39 weeks' pay.[4]

---

1 Case 170/84, [1986] ECR 1607 (ECJ).

2 Arbitration award of 8 December 1977 in the *FDB* case.

3 Arbitration award of 29 April 1987 in the *Premier Is* case.

4 Section 15(2) of Act No 244 of 1989.

3. EQUAL PAY

3.1 PRINCIPLE

Section 1 of the Equal Pay Act, which is intended to implement art. 1 of Directive 75/117/EEC, provides that

> (1) No discrimination on the ground of sex as regards pay may take place in contravention of this Act.
> (2) An employer shall give men and women equal pay, including equal pay conditions, for the same work or work given the same value.
> (3) The evaluation of the value of the work shall take place on the basis of a general evaluation of relevant qualifications and other relevant factors.
> (4) The provisions laid down in this Act shall not apply to the extent that a corresponding obligation to give equal pay arises out of a collective agreement.

Its wording does not expressly refer to the principle of equal pay. There is, however, no doubt that it must be interpreted in line with the directive.

Article 119 of the EEC Treaty requires Member States to ensure and maintain the application of the principle 'that men and women should receive equal pay for equal work'.

According to art. 1 of Directive 75/117/EEC, the principle of equal pay for men and women outlined in art. 119 of the EEC Treaty means, for the same work or for work to which equal value is attributed, the elimination of all discrimination on grounds of sex with regard to all aspects and conditions of remuneration. In particular, where a job classification system is used for determining pay, it must be based on the same criteria for both men and women and so drawn up as to exclude any discrimination on grounds of sex.

Originally, the Equal Pay Act did not mention the concept of work to which equal value is attributed. In 1983, the Commission took infringement proceedings against Denmark under art. 169 of the EEC Treaty on this ground.[1] The Danish Government asserted that Danish law was entirely in conformity with the directive, and stated that the Equal Pay Act was only a secondary guarantor of the principle of equal pay in cases where observance of that principle was not already ensured under collective agreements. Collective agreements, which govern most employment relationships in Denmark, were, according to the Danish Government, based on the principle of equal pay as applying also to work of equal value. All Danish collective agreements on wages provided for equal pay rates for men and women unless the opposite was expressly stated. Respect for the equal pay principle was regarded as an implied term.

---

1 *Commission* v. *Denmark*, Case 143/83, [1985] ECR 427 (ECJ).

The ECJ held that Member States could leave the implementation of the principle of equal pay to collective agreements. That possibility did not, however, discharge them from the obligation of ensuring that all workers were afforded the full protection provided for in the directive. The State guarantee had to cover all cases where effective protection was not ensured by other means, for whatever reason, and in particular cases where the workers in question were not union members, where the sector in question was not covered by a collective agreement or where such an agreement did not fully guarantee the principle of equal pay.

In that respect the Equal Pay Act did not exhibit the clarity and precision necessary for the protection of the workers concerned. Even accepting the assertions of the Danish Government that the principle of equal pay for men and women, in the broad sense required by the directive, was implemented in collective agreements, it had not been shown that the same implementation of that principle was guaranteed for workers whose rights were not defined in such agreements. The principles of legal certainty and the protection of individuals required an unequivocal wording which would give the persons concerned a clear and precise understanding of their rights and obligations and would enable the courts to ensure that those rights and obligations were observed. The wording of the Danish law did not fulfil those conditions, in as much as it set out the principle of equal pay without referring to work of equal value, thus restricting the scope of the principle. The fact that the Danish Government, in the explanatory remarks attached to the draft Equal Treatment Act, stated that the expression 'same work' was intended to cover 'work to which equal value is attributed' was not sufficient to ensure that the persons concerned were adequately informed. The relevance of those considerations was not affected by the fact that during the preparatory work which led to the adoption of Directive 75/117/EEC the Danish Government entered a declaration in the Council minutes to the effect that 'Denmark is of the view that the expression "same work" can continue to be used in the context of Danish labour law'.

The ECJ has consistently held that such unilateral declarations cannot be relied upon for the interpretation of EC measures, since the objective scope of rules laid down by the common institutions cannot be modified by reservations or objections which Member States may have made at the time the rules were being formulated.

3.2 EXCEPTIONS

The Equal Pay Act provides for no exceptions from the equal pay principle on grounds of the size of the establishment, work being done outside the jurisdiction, health and safety, national security, religion, retirement age or any other ground.

However, s. 5 of the Salaried Employees Act limits the entitlement to sick pay to salaried employees with at least 15 hours work per week. Following the ruling of the ECJ in the *Rinner-Kühn* case,[1] it has been argued[2] in Danish legal literature that this provision is in violation of art. 119 of the EEC Treaty as interpreted in the *Rinner-Kühn* judgment.

3.3 PERSONAL SCOPE OF PRINCIPLE

3.3.1 EMPLOYEES

The continental European countries and the Nordic countries apply a broad concept of 'employment contract', resulting in nearly all persons who are in employment being covered by a contract of employment. The United Kingdom, on the other hand, applies a much narrower concept of the contract of employment. Nearly all statutory employment rights are limited to 'employees' under a 'contract of employment'. The effect is to exclude about one-third of those in employment from protection. It is partly because of the UK definition of employment contract that Directive 77/187/EEC on the safeguarding of employees' rights in the event of transfers of undertakings and Directive 80/987/EEC on the protection of employees in the event of the insolvency of their employer use the words 'contract of employment or employment relationship'. The narrow UK concept of a contract of employment also influences the legal discussion in the EC on the implementation of the Equality Directives, as can be seen from the following extract from a report on the Equality Directives:[3]

> ... The present author believes that the contract of employment is a particularly unsuitable mechanism for drawing the boundaries of the Equality Directives. It is therefore to be recommended that it should not be used as a condition of protection. This may necessitate a new definition of 'employment'.

This problem does not exist in Denmark where the employment contract covers practically all instances of employment.

3.3.2 INDEPENDENT CONTRACTORS

A genuinely independent contractor falls outside the scope of the Equal Pay Act. If such a person is not genuinely independent he or she is covered by the Act. There is no Danish case law on independent contractors in relation to the Equal Pay Act.

---

1 Case 171/88, [1989] ECR 2743 (ECJ).

2 See R. NIELSEN, *Judiciel aktivisme i EF-arbejdsretten*, Retfærd, 1979.

3 F. VON PRONDZYNSKI, Network of Experts on the Implementation of the Equality Directives, *Final Consolidated Report*, 1988, p. 10.

3.3.3 HOME WORKERS

Home workers are covered by the Equal Pay Act.

3.3.4 PUBLIC SECTOR

The Equal Pay Act covers both the private and the public sectors.

3.3.5 DOMESTIC EMPLOYEES

Domestic employees are covered by the Equal Pay Act.

3.3.6 NON-EMPLOYED POPULATION

The Equal Pay Act covers paid employment only.

3.4 ACTIVITIES COVERED

All paid activities are covered by the Equal Pay Act.

3.5 DEFINITION OF REMUNERATION

3.5.1 ARTICLE 119 OF THE EEC TREATY

For the purpose of art. 119 of the EEC Treaty, 'pay' means the ordinary basic or minimum wage or salary and any other consideration, whether in cash or in kind, which the worker receives, directly or indirectly, in respect of his employment from his employer. Equal pay without discrimination based on sex means:

(a) that pay for the same work at piece rate shall be calculated on the basis of the same unit of measurement;
(b) that pay for work at time rates shall be the same for the same job.

According to art. 1 of Directive 75/117/EEC, the principle of equal pay for men and women outlined in art. 119 of the EEC Treaty means, for the same work or for work to which equal value is attributed, the elimination of all discrimination on grounds of sex with regard to all aspects and conditions of remuneration. In particular, where a job classification system is used for determining pay, it must be based on the same criteria for both men and women and so drawn up as to exclude any discrimination on grounds of sex.

In the *Defrenne-III* case,[1] the applicant attempted to invoke art. 119 of the EEC Treaty against a discriminatory term in her contract relating to dismissal. Female employees' contracts were terminated when they reached the age of 40, whereas men doing the same work could continue in

1 Case 149/77, [1978] ECR 1365 (ECJ).

employment past this age. The treatment she received was in clear violation of art. 5 of Directive 76/207/EEC, but it occurred before the coming into force of that directive. She therefore tried to obtain an interpretation of art. 119 of the EEC Treaty which extended it to cover discriminatory contractual working conditions. The United Kingdom Equal Pay Act 1970 covers all contractual terms and conditions, not just pay. The ECJ refused to extend the scope of art. 119 to all contractual matters and held that it only applied to pay.

In Denmark, it is the general view that remuneration under Danish law has the same meaning as under EC law.

3.5.2 FRINGE BENEFITS

In *Garland* v. *British Rail Engineering Ltd*,[1] the ECJ ruled that travel concessions offered by British Rail to former employees constituted pay within the meaning of art. 119 of the EEC Treaty. British Rail allowed the families of retired male employees to benefit from rail-fare reductions; this benefit was not extended to the families of retired female employees. The ECJ held that this was discrimination on grounds of sex falling within the scope of art. 119 of the EEC Treaty.

In Denmark there has been a similar case in which a private rail company in Jutland offered free travel to the spouses and children of male employees, but not to the families of female employees. The case was settled under the Equal Treatment Act as a problem relating to discriminatory working conditions, not under the Equal Pay Act. The result would have been the same had the Equal Pay Act been used.

3.5.3 CONTRIBUTORY SYSTEMS

In *Worringham* v. *Lloyds Bank Ltd*,[2] the ECJ held that contributions included in the calculation of a gross salary constituted pay within the meaning of art. 119(2) of the EEC Treaty, even if they were immediately deducted and paid into a pension fund on behalf of the employee. This interpretation is generally accepted in Denmark.

3.5.4 PENSIONS

In *Defrenne-I*,[3] the ECJ held that a statutory retirement pension financed by contributions from workers, employers and by State subsidy falls outside the terms of art. 119 of the EEC Treaty. Applied to Danish law, this judgment means that the Danish labour market supplementary pension

1 Case 12/81, [1982] ECR 359 (ECJ).

2 Case 69/80, [1981] ECR 767 (ECJ).

3 Case 80/70, [1971] ECR 445 (ECJ).

(*arbejdsmarkedets tillægspension*) falls outside the scope of the equal pay provisions and falls to be considered instead under Directive 79/7/EEC. The part-time criterion is used in this pension system in a way that may be indirectly discriminatory in violation of art. 4 of Directive 79/7/EEC, as interpreted in the *Ruzius-Wilbrink* case.[1]

3.5.5 COLLECTIVE AGREEMENTS

All Danish collective agreements on wages provide for equal pay for men and women unless the opposite is expressly stated. Respect for the equal pay principle is regarded as an implied term. This interpretation is supported by the mediation proposal of 28 March 1973, which abolished different pay rates for men and women in collective agreements between members of LO and DA (the two main organizations) as of 1 April 1973 (i.e. three months after art. 119 of the EEC Treaty, according to the *Defrenne-II* judgment, became directly effective in Denmark).

In practice there are never express clauses providing for unequal pay. In 1989 a survey of Danish collective agreements was conducted for a project exploring the setting up of a database on collective agreements affecting women and work.[2] This did not find any express clauses providing for unequal pay. It did not find any express equal pay clauses either. This is in accordance with the general expert view that such clauses probably do not exist in Denmark. The description of the Danish collective agreement protection of the equal pay principle, according to the Report of the Commission of the European Communities on the application of this principle[3] where it is maintained that it should be considered necessary in Denmark to insert equal pay clauses into collective agreements, is perhaps somewhat misleading. There is no need for express clauses, as there is always an implied clause.

Since Danish collective agreement equal pay clauses are implied, they do not contribute to the definition of the concept of remuneration. Different wage systems are used in Denmark. In the normal wage system, workers receive the rates laid down in the collective agreement and nothing more. In the minimum wage system, the collective agreement lays down the minimum wage. Most workers or employees receive increments based on a very wide variety of criteria. There is no doubt that both the rates laid down in collective agreements and the increments attached to them in the minimum wage system are pay which must comply with the equal pay principle; but it is controversial as to what extent the criteria for receiving increments are indirectly discriminatory and to what extent the burden of proof should be on

---

1 Case C-102/88, [1989] ECR 4311 (ECJ).

2 R. NIELSEN and A. REINERT, *Feasibility of a European Database on Women and Work*, Danish Report, Copenhagen, 1989.

3 COM(78) 711, p. 57 and in particular p. 58.

the employer when he uses the minimum wage system, which in some instances is not transparent (see §6.1.2 below). The general pattern is that male-dominated groups get more additional payments than predominantly female groups, a fact which makes it likely that this wage system serves as a cover for indirect discrimination.

3.6 COMPARATOR

In the case of sex discrimination based on the multi-variable, biological gender concept or the social gender concept, there is no need for a woman to find a male comparator. In Danish legal literature it has, for example, been argued that pregnant women receive sick pay subject to more stringent conditions than others.[1] If this is the case, it is a violation of the equal pay principle irrespective of whether it happens in a woman-only workplace or in a situation where comparisons with men could be made. If part-time workers were paid less per hour than full-time workers, it would be a contravention of the equal pay principle without there being any need for a male comparator.

In *Macarthys Ltd* v. *Smith*,[2] a female stockroom manager was paid less than her male predecessor. The ECJ was asked whether art. 119 of the EEC Treaty applied to a comparison with a predecessor, and also if Directive 75/117/EEC, as well as art. 119, was directly effective. The court ruled that art. 119 of the EEC Treaty was directly applicable to comparisons between a woman and her male predecessor, and did not therefore answer the question concerning the direct applicability of Directive 75/117/EEC. There have been no similar cases in Denmark. The *Macarthys* case is referred to in the most widely used commentary on Danish equality legislation as an expression of the law currently in force.[3]

In an equal pay case against the Danish Cremation Society,[4] consideration was given to the question of the scope of permissible comparisons. In this case the work of two female salaried employees was compared with that of a former male colleague during a period of about two and a half years. They were all paid according to a minimum wage agreement between HK and DA. The two women were employed, respectively, in November 1979 and December 1983 to arrange removals to the mortuary in two different district offices. The man was employed in December 1984 to arrange removals to the mortuary in 'our offices', based at the main office. The contracts of employment were thus in identical terms as far as work was concerned. Both women worked when needed as substitutes

---

1 See A. ANDERSEN and R. NIELSEN, *Ligestillingslovene med kommentarer*, 2nd edition, Copenhagen, 1990.

2 Case 129/79, [1980] ECR 1275 (ECJ).

3 See A. ANDERSEN and R. NIELSEN, *op. cit.*

4 *HK mod DA for Dansk Ligbrændingsforening Begravelsesforetningen Danmark*, arbitration award of 25 April 1990, unreported.

in other district offices. Furthermore, one woman worked as a substitute for half a year in the man's job. The man was to work as substitute according to need in all district offices. The employers gave information during the case that when the man was recruited it was stated that he was also to deputise in provincial offices, in the transport department and as home arranger. HK disputed this.

While considering the identical contracts of employment the arbitrator found that they entailed the same work or work of equal value. However he emphasized that the man actually had further tasks which he was obliged to carry out and ruled that, in the light of the type of work and the nature of the availability obligation, it followed from an overall assessment that the man's work was of higher value than that of the women. The presumption of equal value which the identical contracts of employment could lead to was not used, as the arbitrator in his assessment of the evidence did not have information about the character of the work in the transport department, and also as there was contradictory evidence about the extent to which the job included tasks other than the ones mentioned in the contract of employment from the beginning. Furthermore, the two women's experience in the job was not taken into account in the overall assessment of the value of the job. Against this background the ruling should not become a precedent.

In a case involving the Danish Clothing and Textile Workers' Union,[1] the union claimed that the value of the work performed in the burls by unskilled women was of the same value as the work 10 unskilled men performed in weaving. The additional payment claimed included a five-year period, calculated from the time the union raised the claim. Both groups were paid according to a fixed hourly rate according to the same normal wage agreement. The men operated the weaving machines and the women did burl work, i.e. checking and correcting mistakes in machine-made carpets. To a certain extent both groups assisted each other.

A description of work from a former leader of the Danish Clothing and Textile Institute (*Dansk Beklædnings- og Tekstilinstitut*) and a statement from the Equal Status Council were considered in the Arbitration Tribunal. Contrary to the recommendation of the Council the arbitrator ruled that weaving work was considered to be of higher value than the burl work and emphasized that the weavers had to operate valuable machines, that the quality of their work determined the requirement for later burling of the carpets, that the weavers had more work than the burl workers, and that their training time was longer than that of the burl workers. The last condition was denied by the trade union.

---

1 *Dansk Beklædnings- og Tekstilarbejderforbund mod Tekstilindustrien for Hammer Tæpper A/S, Herning*, arbitration award of 12 October 1990, unreported.

The arbitrator chose to disregard the fact that both types of work were unskilled, that according to the local agreement both men and women received lower starting wages for a period of three months for new employees, and that both types of work were a step in the same process of work. The choice of criteria of job evaluation in the decision lacked detailed grounds and therefore it could be said to be unsuitable as a precedent.

Another case concerned the different wages of unskilled women and men, in that the firm paid lower starting wages to the 40 unskilled women, and only the 40 unskilled men were paid a seniority allowance.[1] The collective claim for payment in arrears included the agreement period in which the claim was made. Both groups were paid in accordance with the collective agreement on minimum wages of the Confederation of Danish Industry (*Dansk Industri*), and also in accordance with two different local agreements which fixed lower starting wages for women than men and gave only men seniority allowances. The two groups took care of selected sections of the total process of production of tightening systems, in such a way that the main tasks of the men were in production while the women took care of the finishing treatment, packing, marking and final checking.

The arbitrator agreed with the trade union with reference to the 'extent and nature' of the work of the women, and that it was not critical that the work of the women was completely different from that of the men and took place in departments where only women were employed. The arbitrator said that the seniority allowances for the men appeared to amount to clearly unfair treatment and had no relevant operational reasons, and that it was a violation of the Equal Pay Act.

The ruling did not give any reasons for the job evaluation contained in it, which is comparable to the one in the *FDB* case,[2] and which seems to be far broader than the one undertaken in the case of *Hammer Tæpper.* With the clarification of certain issues relevant to seniority allowances and the employers' burden of proof, the ruling marked a further development in the guidelines arising out of the ECJ's ruling in the *Danfoss* case.

In another case,[3] unskilled men and women were paid according to a normal wage agreement, and additionally received two personal allowances fixed according to a local agreement. The women machine operators operated the machines which produced plastic packing and packed the finished products on pallets, while the shop foreman assistants supplied the machines with raw goods and drove the pallets with finished goods to the

1 *Kvindeligt Arbejderforbund i Danmark mod W.S. Shamban Europa A/S, Helsingør,* arbitration award of 6 March 1991, unreported.

2 Arbitration award of 8 December 1977.

3 *Kvindeligt Arbejderforbund i Danmark mod R. Færch Plast A/S*, arbitration award of 5 July 1991, unreported.

stores. To a certain extent shop foreman assistants were substitutes for the machine operators and maintained the higher wages during this work. It took the arbitrator 10 months to make a ruling, and he emphasized that the shop foreman assistants' choice of raw materials determined the production as a whole. *KAD* stated that the arbitrator had misunderstood the facts of the case which he had chosen to emphasise. For this reason, and because the ruling did not explain the choice of criteria for job evaluation and also did not deal with the submission of the trade union on the burden of proof, it probably should not become a precedent.

In *HK for Winnie Bradstrup* v. *the Employers' Association for Butchers for Steff-Houlberg Slagterierne A.m.b.A., Ringsted department*, the duties of two office clerks employed in the supervisory department of the slaughterhouse were compared. The trade union's claim included the payment of arrears according to the five year rule in the Prescription Act, calculated from the moment when the union raised the claim against the employers' union until the moment when the woman was dismissed. The two employees were paid according to a minimum wage agreement. The woman had undergone vocational training as a clerk with office practice at the firm and had 11 years' seniority, whereas the man was unskilled and had 12 years' seniority doing various duties. The two employees shared an office, there was no fixed division of labour between them, and they covered for each other in the case of an absence.

The arbitrator ruled that the additional tasks given to the man during the case were partly of less value and partly outweighed by the fact that for several years the woman had been in charge of training apprentices. Against this background the work could be of equal value, so the burden of proof was on the employer. The employer had explained that the reason for the difference in wages was the greater initiative of the man, his flexibility and seniority. The first two criteria mentioned were, without any explanation, considered as not proven. The seniority criterion was not accepted as a reasonable ground since the difference was of no importance after the employment period of about 10 years and as this ground was first put forward during the arbitration hearing.

This ruling applied a detailed job evaluation, and it was the first which found in favour of an employee in the field of minimum wages. It was also the first directly to use the burden of proof rule which the ECJ established in the *Danfoss* case. In the equal pay field the ruling was the first to emphasize that the usual five-year time limit is valid in cases of this kind.

In *HK mod DA for Danfoss A/S, Sønderjylland*, the HK claimed that on average the male employees at *Danfoss* covered by the minimum wage agreement were paid higher wages than the women, and that this difference in pay was inconsistent with the Equal Pay Act. The HK submitted that the employers had the onus of proving that their payment policy was not in violation of the Act. During the case the arbitration tribunal decided to submit to the ECJ a number of preliminary questions.

The claim concerned about 400 persons, of whom about 80 per cent were women. During the preparation of the case the parties brought forward detailed statistical evidence to illustrate that the wage difference was related to sex. This resulted in agreement that there was an average difference in wages to the detriment of women, while there remained disagreement as to its size.

Based on the decision of the ECJ in the case the arbitrators ruled that the wage system at issue was totally lacking in transparency, and thus the burden of proof was on the firm to show that the wage difference was not unlawful. The ruling did not stipulate a specific amount of back pay and probably, in the context of the claim, did not have the possibility of doing so, but it ordered the firm to correct the wages within two months. Finally the ruling clarified that there was a general duty on employers to give information in order to ensure the effectiveness of the equal pay principle as required by EC law. The ruling is fundamental both in its presentation and its consistent and direct use of the principles of interpretation which the ECJ has established in its decisions. The case was eventually settled by way of a compromise.

3.7 WOMAN DOES SAME WORK AS MAN

If a woman does exactly the same work as a man, it is obvious that she is entitled to equal pay. There are no cases on this situation, which may be because the more crude forms of discrimination have been eliminated in Denmark.

3.8 EQUAL VALUE

3.8.1 JOB EVALUATION

Formal job evaluation schemes are unusual in Denmark. When an equal value claim is made the industrial arbitration tribunal makes an informal assessment of the value of the work. There are two Danish arbitration awards, one from 1977[1] and another from 1987,[2] in which it was held that unskilled male and female workers doing the same work or work of equal value must be paid equal pay. The fact that they are covered by two different collective agreements cannot be used as an excuse for different pay for women and men where the workers are unskilled. In the infringement case[3] taken against Denmark the Danish Government invoked the 1977 award in arguing for the compatibility of Danish law with EC law.

---

1 Arbitration award of 8 December 1977 in the *FDB* case.

2 Arbitration award of 29 April 1987 in the *Premier Is* case.

3 Case 143/83, [1985] ECR 427 (ECJ).

3.8.2 JOB CLASSIFICATION

Some Danish employers covered by minimum wage collective agreements apply job classification schemes. This was the case in *Danfoss*.

In the *Rummler* case,[1] the ECJ ruled that the criteria governing pay classification must ensure that work which is objectively the same attracts the same rate of pay, whether it is performed by a man or a woman. The Court further declared the use of values reflecting the average performance of workers of one sex as a basis for determining the extent to which work makes demands or requires effort or whether it is heavy constitutes a form of discrimination on grounds of sex, contrary to Directive 75/117/EEC. The ECJ stated that in order for a job classification system not to be discriminatory as a whole, it must, in so far as the nature of the tasks carried out in the undertaking permits, take into account criteria for which workers of each sex may show particular aptitude.

3.8.3 HIGHER VALUE AND PROPORTIONATE PAY

To date there has been no case law on whether it is possible to claim proportionate pay.

3.9 LEGITIMATE REASON FOR PAY DIFFERENTIAL

In the *Danfoss* case questions were put regarding the defence an employer can use to discharge the burden of proof. The company applied a collective agreement within the minimum wage system which set basic rates of pay for the various grades of workers, but allowed for individual increments based on flexibility, vocational training and seniority.

The ECJ declared that where an undertaking applied a pay system which was characterized by a total lack of transparency, the burden of proof was on the employer to show that his wage practice was not discriminatory where a female worker established, by comparison with a relatively large number of employees, that the average pay of female workers was lower than that of male workers. The employer could only justify pay differences by reference to vocational training or flexibility if that training or flexibility was relevant to the work as actually performed. The employer could justify pay differences by reference to seniority without having to show why seniority was relevant.

---

1 Case 237/85, [1986] ECR 2101 (ECJ).

In Danish case law prior to the *Danfoss* judgment, in particular in the *Vejle Amts Folkeblad* case,[1] a difference in vocational training was accepted as a defence even though it had no relevance to the work actually performed.

There is no Danish case law on red circles, but the problem has been discussed at an informal level. It seems to be the general view that red circling is not a lawful defence.

1 Arbitration award of 11 February 1985, published in *Arbejdsretligt Tidsskrift*, 1985, p. 185.

4. EQUAL TREATMENT

4.1 PRINCIPLE

According to art. 2(1) of Directive 76/207/EEC, the principle of equal treatment means that there shall be no discrimination on grounds of sex, either directly or indirectly, by reference in particular to marital or family status. The wording of s. 1 of the Equal Treatment Act, which is intended to implement art. 1 of the directive, follows the wording of the directive rather closely. The Equal Treatment Act mentions pregnancy along with marital or family status.

4.2 EXCEPTIONS

4.2.1 EXCLUSIONS

4.2.1.1 Size

The Equal Treatment Act applies to employers irrespective of size.

4.2.1.2 Work done outside the jurisdiction

The first court case[1] under the Equal Treatment Act concerned an applicant who had failed to be appointed to a job as a sailor because she was a woman. The employer rejected the applicant because he had not wanted to employ women as deck-hands on board ships which were to call at ports in the Far East, Singapore etc. The majority considered this a violation of s. 2 of the Equal Treatment Act. In accordance with s. 8 of the Act compensation of DKR 10,000 was awarded.

A commercial company (East Asian Company) has had a four-year exemption from the Equal Treatment Act, allowing it to exclude women from service in the Far East. The exemption has expired and has not been renewed.[2]

4.2.1.3 Health and safety

In one case,[3] a shipping company had refused to hire a woman sailor because their ship had no separate washroom with a bathroom for women. The majority of judges (four judges) in the Supreme Court (*Højesteret*)

---

1 U 1980, 328.

2 See *Ligestillingrådets Årsberetning,* 1984, 51.

3 U 1980, 569.

considered that the shipping company had violated s. 2 of the Equal Treatment Act. No compensation was awarded.

4.2.1.4 Security

See §4.2.2.4 below.

4.2.1.5 Retirement age

Sex-based differences in retirement age are in violation of the Equal Treatment Act.

4.2.2 SEX AS A DETERMINING FACTOR

4.2.2.1 Lists

In connection with the adoption of the Equal Treatment Act in 1978 the Ministry of Labour in the explanatory remarks[1] expressed the view that a number of jobs fall outside the scope of the Act because, due to their nature, they must be performed either by a man or a woman, for example jobs as actors, bathing personnel or models.

These exceptions are not explicitly mentioned in the Act, but the Equal Treatment Act is not intended to apply to such situations. Danish courts usually interpret an Act in accordance with the explanatory remarks. This means that there is a very imprecise general exclusion of cases where sex is a determining factor in the Equal Treatment Act. If an employer thinks he needs specifically a man or a woman he can use this exception at his own discretion. There is no official list of what comes under this exception. It is therefore only possible to give examples (e.g. models, actors, bathing personnel). In addition, Denmark has done nothing to meet its obligations under art. 9(2) of Directive 76/207/EEC.

A rejected applicant who believes she or he has been discriminated against in an unlawful way will have to bring proceedings before the courts, who will then have the final say as to whether or not sex was a genuine occupational qualification. Such cases are never brought in practice. If they were the Danish courts would probably follow the explanatory remarks to the Act. It is, however, also possible that they would refer such cases to the ECJ under art. 177 of the EEC Treaty in order to clarify the legal position under EC law on this point.

---

1 *Folketingstidende, Tillæg A*, 1977-78, sp 3088.

4.2.2.2 Genuine occupational qualification[1]

Under s. 13(1)[2] of the Equal Treatment Act the Ministry under whose authority a particular kind of work falls can grant exemption from the Act when the sex of the worker is a determining factor.

The borderline between the above-mentioned exception in the explanatory remarks to the Equal Treatment Act and the explicit exceptions under s. 13(1) of the Act is blurred. In practice it is a question of how obvious the employer believes the case to be and of how law-abiding he is. If the employer either believes it to be obvious that sex is a determining factor or if he doesn't care whether or not he is violating the Act he will tend to act without asking for an exemption. If he believes the case to be dubious, or if he is more law-abiding, he will apply for an exemption under s. 13(1).

The Ministry of Industry has refused to grant an exemption for a training ship on which seafarers are trained. The Ministry of the Interior has refused to give an exemption to a psychiatric hospital which thought that men only should be employed at work where there is a risk of the patients committing violence against the personnel.

4.2.2.3 Authenticity

See 4.2.2.1 above.

4.2.2.4 Security

A project concerning the integration of women in the combat troops of the Army and the Air Force was completed in 1987. A similar project concerning the Naval Forces was completed in 1985. Following the pilot schemes to integrate women into the different military services, women now have access to all military functions with the exception of fighter pilot. The armed forces obtained a dispensation from the Equal Treatment Act for the latter, since the physical effects of strong acceleration in a fighter aircraft on women are uncertain. A number of medical examinations in relation to flying will therefore be carried out before a decision as to whether women can become fighter pilots can be reached.

The Ministry of Defence has exempted positions involving active combat. Small projects regarding women in military functions have been

---

1 See R. NIELSEN, 'Equality in Working Life: Legislation, Positive Action and Introduction of New Technology', in 'Women's Law in Scandinavia', *European Women's Law*, No 1, 1982, col. 112-114.

2 Formerly s. 11(1) of the Act.

launched with a view to improving women's job opportunities in the military in the future.[1]

4.2.2.5 Religion

Section 11(1) of the Equal Treatment Act has been used by the Ministry of Churches to allow recognized religious communities to decide for themselves whether or not they will accept women priests.

4.2.2.6 Decency and privacy

The Ministry of Education has granted an exemption allowing preference to be given to male applicants for vocational training as interpreters for the deaf; the reason is that there are not enough male applicants with the level of qualifications required to produce a sufficient number of male interpreters to allow the clients a free choice between male and female interpreters. Interpreters for the deaf assist clients in various situations, for example when visiting a doctor, and it is regarded as desirable that a deaf man can choose a male interpreter if he so wishes.[2]

4.2.2.7 Single-sex establishments

The Ministry of Social Affairs has granted exemption allowing a crisis centre for battered women to employ women only.[3]

4.3 TERRITORIAL SCOPE

The Equal Treatment Act applies to all work to which Danish law applies under the choice-of-law rules of private international law.

4.4 PERSONAL SCOPE

The Equal Treatment Act covers the same categories as the Equal Pay Act. In addition it covers access to independent professions and vocational training.

4.5 ACTIVITIES COVERED

All activities carried out by an employer in his capacity as employer are covered by the Equal Treatment Act. In addition, the Act covers access to independent professions and vocational training. Trade union activities fall outside the scope of the Equal Treatment Act. Denmark has a women-only

---

1 See *Ligestillingsrådets Årsberetning,* 1981, p. 194. See on a project on the police *Ligestillingsrådets Årsberetning* 1977, p. 195.

2 See *Ligestillingsrådets Årsberetning,* 1987, p. 77.

3 See *Ligestillingsrådets Årsberetning,* 1985, p. 83.

trade union (*Kvindeligt Arbejderforbund*) for various categories of unskilled women workers. Unskilled male workers doing the same work (or work of equal value) will be members of another, male-dominated, union (SiD). Sex discrimination resulting from the sex-based structure of the trade unions is not covered by the Equal Treatment Act or any other Danish provision on equality.

4.6 COMPARATOR

In the case of sex discrimination based on the multi-variable, biological gender concept, there is no need for an individual woman to find an individual male comparator. In the case of indirect discrimination, the relevant comparison will be between groups of women and groups of men.

4.7 HIRING

4.7.1 RECRUITMENT METHODS

Under Danish law the employer is generally free to choose recruitment methods, such as advertisements, or internal as against external recruitment. In a workplace dominated by one sex internal recruitment may be considered indirectly discriminatory.

It is a violation of the prohibition against indirect discrimination if the employer imposes requirements which are not obviously relevant to the job and only serve as a pretext for attracting applicants of a particular sex. One can mention as examples cases where the employer requires the successful applicant, for a job as a salesperson, to be at least 1.77 m tall, or for a job as supervisor in a textile factory to have detailed knowledge in theory and practice of football.

4.7.2 ADVERTISEMENTS

It is a violation of the prohibition against direct discrimination where, for example, the employer explicitly asks in a job advertisement for women or men, or if persons who respond to a neutral job advertisement are told by telephone that only women or men are wanted for the job in question. There is a criminal sanction (a fine) for discriminatory job advertisements. It is, however, lawful to encourage women specifically to apply.[1]

4.7.3 JOB TITLE

It is unlawful and results in a fine if a gender-related job title is used in situations where a gender-neutral title exists.

---

1 Labour Ministry Statutory Instrument (*Arbejdsministeriets bekendtgørelse*) No 757 of 1989.

4.7.4 JOB DESCRIPTION

The job description must be gender-neutral.

4.7.5 SELECTION ARRANGEMENTS

It is unlawful to ask woman applicants if they are pregnant. There have been no Danish cases on discriminatory selection arrangements.

4.7.6 TERMS ON WHICH A JOB IS OFFERED

It is probably by and large easier for women than for men to get part-time jobs. This is in violation of the equal treatment principle.

In one case,[1] a male student who wanted to work part-time as an unskilled worker took proceedings against his union (SiD) and his employer because the collective agreement did not allow part-time work. Had he been a woman he would have belonged to the Women Workers' Union (*Kvindeligt Arbejderforbund*) whose collective agreement covering the same work allowed part-time work. The court found that the collective agreement arrangement as a whole was incompatible with the Equal Treatment Act, but the court did not find that the 'male' collective agreement seen in isolation was in contravention of the Act and therefore invalid. The plaintiff consequently lost his case. In Denmark there are different opinions as to whether it is favourable or unfavourable for workers when the collective agreement allows the employer to operate part-time employment. In the above case the 'male' union claimed that their collective agreement was better than the female collective agreement; if one of the collective agreements was invalid, it was argued that this should be the women's agreement.

4.7.7 REFUSAL OR DELIBERATE OMISSION TO OFFER A JOB

The prohibition against direct discrimination can be violated by omissions as well as by actions. An employer who advertises a job vacancy and gets many applicants of whom the best qualified are of a particular sex commits direct sex discrimination if, in order to avoid hiring them, he does not fill the job.[2]

---

1 U 1982, 484.

2 For a possible example of such discrimination see the annual report of the Equal Status Council, 1985, p. 70, concerning a woman who did not become a conductor at the Royal Life Guard.

4.8 WORKING CONDITIONS

In Denmark there has been a case, similar to *Garland* v. *British Rail Engineering Ltd*,[1] where a private rail company in Jutland offered free travels to the spouses and children of male employees but not to the families of female employees. The case was settled under the Equal Treatment Act as relating to discriminatory working conditions, not under the Equal Pay Act. The result would have been the same had the Equal Pay Act been used.

Sexual harassment is, as mentioned, prohibited by the Equal Treatment Act (see §2.2.2.2 above). This follows from case law[2] and is also the general view of legal writers.[3]

4.9 EXCLUSION, DISMISSAL OR OTHER DETRIMENT

A case relevant to this heading concerned a factory where unskilled men and women workers did the same work (or work of equal value).[4] They were covered by a joint collective agreement between, on the one hand, the employer, and on the other hand, the two sex-segregated trade unions for unskilled workers (*Kvindeligt Arbejderforbund* and SiD). Until 1976 they had been covered by two separate collective agreements. The joint agreement contained a provision enabling the employer to send workers home without pay in certain situations if they were doing work which before 1976 had been covered by the collective agreement with the Women Workers' Union. In the same situations workers who did work which before 1976 was covered by the collective agreement with the male-dominated union could not be sent home without pay. It was beyond dispute that in practice nearly everyone working under the unfavourable provision in the agreement were women and nearly everyone covered by the more favourable provision were men. The Women Workers' Union (*Kvindeligt Arbejderforbund*) claimed that the collective agreement was incompatible with the Equal Treatment Act and consequently partly invalid.

The majority in the Supreme Court found that there was no discrimination in the wording of the collective agreement and therefore no violation of the Equal Treatment Act. In principle men could do work which before 1976 was covered by the agreement with the Women Workers' Union and women could do work which before 1976 was covered by the agreement with the male-dominated union. In practice they did not. The minority in the Supreme Court found that the Equal Treatment Act had been violated.

---

1 Case 12/81, [1982] ECR 359 (ECJ).

2 Judgment of 8 September 1989 by Østre Landsret, 4. *afdeling* a s 262/1988, *Vibeke Rønn mod SiD, Fåborg Afdeling*.

3 H. PETERSEN, 'Retsbeskyttelse af kvinders værdighed', *TFR*, 1988, p. 253.

4 U 1983, 379.

4.10 INSTRUCTIONS TO DISCRIMINATE

Instructions and pressure to discriminate are unlawful. Discrimination by an employee is covered by the Equal Treatment Act (see §2.2.2.2 above).

4.11 PRESSURE TO DISCRIMINATE

See §4.10 above.

4.12 DISCRIMINATION BY AN EMPLOYEE OR A TRADE UNION

See §4.10 above.

4.13 DISCRIMINATORY PRACTICES

There have been no Danish cases on discriminatory practices. Such practices are unlawful.

4.14 SPECIAL TREATMENT

4.14.1 PROTECTIVE LEGISLATION

Denmark has, as mentioned in the introduction, a strong tradition of not providing special protection for women.[1]

4.14.1.1 Pregnancy and maternity

Dismissal on grounds of pregnancy or parental leave is prohibited by the Equal Treatment Act. There are a number of cases dealing with the dismissal of pregnant women.

In 1987 the Equal Status Council attempted to promote greater understanding for a rather rare disease. This disease, which causes the floor and the bones of the pelvis to loosen, develops during pregnancy. A case was brought to test whether it was a violation of the Equal Treatment Act to dismiss an employee absent for a long period because of illness resulting from this disease. Questions concerning the interpretation of Directive 76/207/EEC in this respect were put to the ECJ.[2]

---

1 See R. NIELSEN, 'Special protective legislation for women in the Nordic countries', in *International Labour Review*, vol. 119, No 1, Geneva, 1980.

2 *Handels- og Kontorfunktionærernes Forbund i Danmark (Birte Vibeke Hertz)* v. *Dansk Arbejdsgiverforening (Aldi Marked K/S)*, Case C-179/88, [1990] ECR I-3979 (ECJ).

4.14.2 POSITIVE ACTION

By virtue of the amendment to the Equal Treatment Act in 1989 the Equal Status Council was given the power to permit positive action exemptions.[1] In pursuance of the 1989 amendment in the Equal Treatment Act, a statutory instrument was issued in December 1989 permitting positive action in relation to training.[2]

4.14.2.1 Definition

The term positive action is usually given a broad meaning in the Scandinavian countries, comprising a number of measures to promote equality between the sexes, such as:[3]

- sex quotas;
- preferential access to training and jobs for members of the under-represented sex;
- different requirements (e.g. different height requirements) for women and men;
- special supportive measures for either men or women;
- courses to help women enter occupations in which they have traditionally been under-represented;
- special guidance and support during training which members of one sex have tended to find difficult to complete;
- subsidies to employers who hire men or women in jobs not common for their sex;
- a duty to ensure that both women and men are considered seriously when vacancies, posts in committees etc. are filled. This can for example be implemented by requiring that nominations for these positions include at least a man and a woman;
- active recruitment, in the form of special approaches to members of the under-represented sex to encourage them to apply;
- stipulation of goals and timetables.

In cases where it is regarded as undesirable to use the above methods of positive action, or where it is decided to combine different forms of positive action, it is common to lay down a policy goal, for example that women's share of training or an occupation shall amount to a certain percentage within two years.

---

1 Section 13(2)-(4) of Act No 244 of 1989.

2 Labour Ministry Statutory Instrument (*Arbejdsministeriets bekendtgørelse*) No 757 of 1989.

3 See for example 'En vej til ligestilling — positiv særbehandling,' *Udvalget vedrørende kønsroller og uddannelse*, No 4, Ministry of Education, Copenhagen, 1982.

Influencing opinion in favour of equality is not usually included in the concept of positive action. 'Structural changes', such as changes in age requirements, provision of childcare facilities, or changes in educational or training requirements, may, due to the different social situation of the sexes, benefit women more than men. They are usually considered separately from positive action.

4.14.2.2 Areas

Training bodies

Positive action exemptions have primarily been granted to enable public authorities to organize women-only courses and employment projects as part of the public policy efforts to combat unemployment, particularly youth unemployment. In the amendment to the Equal Treatment Act of 1989 a general exemption was inserted for training.[1]

Employers

So far, only a few employers, both in the public and private sector, have shown any interest in applying for permission to take positive action measures. The freedom they had to take positive action measures before the Act was passed had also been rarely used.

4.14.2.3 Means

Some of the examples listed above involve discrimination within the meaning of the prohibition of discrimination. This applies, for example, to sex quotas and preferential access to jobs for the under-represented sex. Other positive action measures are not affected by the prohibition of discrimination under the existing equality laws. This applies, for example, to policy goals concerning equality.

It is also possible for public bodies, employers and others to develop their expertise in matters of women's employment without authorization, and, for example, to set up special committees or employ staff with specialist knowledge in this field. Equal opportunities consultants were introduced in the Danish public labour market administration in 1981. Their tasks are:

- to ensure that the work of the public employment service is based on the principle of equal opportunities for men and women and reflects this attitude. It is therefore the duty of the consultant to instruct, counsel and advise the staff in this field;

---

1 Labour Ministry Statutory Instrument (*Arbejdsministeriets bekendtgørelse*) No 757 of 1989.

- to take part in developing methods of communication and guidance aimed at changing the traditional way of thinking as regards men and women's qualifications and opportunities in the labour market (which is to be found among employers as well as workers);
- to take part in launching experiments which may increase the amount of knowledge of how women and men deal with non-traditional occupations;
- to take part in the organizing and evaluation of training and employment measures on the basis of the principle of equality of opportunity.

The equal opportunities consultants are attached to the regional employment services.[1]

4.14.2.4 Constitutional or legal problems

Since there are no provisions on equality in the Danish Constitution, positive action does not give rise to constitutional problems.

A shift seems to have occurred during the 1980s in the interpretation of the relationship between positive action and the prohibition of discrimination. Where the prevailing view in the early and mid-1970s among equality experts was that these measures were incompatible with equality, the prevailing view now is that they are complementary.

---

1 See for a more detailed account L. VALBJØRN 'Equal Opportunities Consultants in the Danish Public Employment Service', in K. HVIDTFELDT, *et al.* (eds), *Strategies for integrating women into the labour market,* Copenhagen, 1982, p. 289 *et seq.*

5. SOCIAL SECURITY

5.1 DEFINITION OF SOCIAL SECURITY

5.1.1 STATUTORY SOCIAL SECURITY

The purpose of Directive 79/7/EEC is the progressive implementation, in the field of social security and other elements of social protection, of the principle of equal treatment for men and women. The directive applies to statutory schemes which provide protection against the following risks:

- sickness,
- invalidity,
- old age,
- accidents at work and occupational diseases,
- unemployment,

and to social assistance, in so far as it is intended to supplement or replace the schemes referred to above.

The directive does not deal with survivors' benefits or family benefits, except in the case of family benefits granted by way of increases of benefits due in respect of the risks referred to in art. 1(a).

Danish social security legislation covers all the subjects mentioned in Directive 79/7/EEC, such as daily allowances in case of illness or confinement, national sickness insurance, invalidity pensions, old-age pensions, insurance against accidents at work, social assistance, supplementary pensions for employees and unemployment insurance. The legislation is mainly financed through taxation. Old-age and invalidity pensions are not as a rule linked to participation in the labour market.

As mentioned previously (see §1.1.2 above), the socio-economic reality is that women in Denmark by and large live under the same dual maintenance system, based on employment and public maintenance, as men. The general principle is that all Danes have an individual right to social security, not a family-derived or family-related right. There are consequently only examples of discrimination in Danish social security law stemming from gender-related differences in the role of the family as a maintenance institution.

The main example of remaining family-related discrimination is an Act from 1941,[1] which provides for the retention of a right to a pension by a

---

1 *Lov nr. 102 af 1941 om bevarelse af enkepensionsret ved separation og skilsmisse*, Act No 102 of 1941 on Retention of Pension Rights after Separation or Divorce.

widow of a deceased civil servant whom she has divorced. A man in the same circumstances has no right to a pension.

The greatest discrimination problem in Danish social security legislation relates to the use of the part-time criterion, which is applied in the unemployment legislation and the Labour Market Supplementary Pensions Act.

5.1.2 OCCUPATIONAL SOCIAL SECURITY

According to art. 2 of Directive 86/378/EEC, occupational social security schemes mean schemes not governed by Directive 79/7/EEC whose purpose is to provide workers, whether employees or self-employed, in an undertaking or group of undertakings, an area of economic activity or occupational sector or group of such sectors, with benefits intended to supplement the benefits provided by statutory social security schemes or to replace them, whether membership of such schemes is compulsory or optional.

Directive 86/378/EEC applies to occupational schemes which provide protection against the risks of sickness, invalidity, old age (including early retirement), industrial accidents and occupational diseases, and unemployment. It also applies to occupational schemes which provide for other social benefits, in cash or in kind, and in particular survivors' benefits and family allowances, if such benefits are accorded to employed persons and thus constitute a consideration paid by the employer to the worker by reason of the latter's employment.

The directive does not apply to:

- individual contracts;
- schemes having only one member;
- in the case of salaried workers, insurance contracts to which the employer is not a party;
- the optional provisions of occupational schemes offered to participants individually to guarantee them either additional benefits, or a choice of date on which the normal benefits will start, or a choice between several benefits.

In Denmark, various social security issues may be dealt with by collective agreement. In practice there are collective agreement provisions on parental leave, sick pay and pensions for some groups of employees.

The Act of 1941[1] referred to above (see §5.1.1 above) is probably in contravention of Directive 86/378/EEC. The same applies to all pension schemes contained in collective agreements which build on the principles of

---

1 Act No 102 of 1941.

this Act. The question as to whether the 1941 Act should be repealed has been a subject of discussion for years.

5.1.3 SOCIAL ASSISTANCE

Social assistance, in so far as it is intended to supplement or replace the schemes referred to in Directive 79/7/EEC, is covered by the directive. In Denmark, social assistance is means-tested. The principle is that all the circumstances of the applicant are taken into account, and the existence of a spouse who could support the applicant is therefore relevant. There is no different treatment of men and women in this respect.

5.1.4 PERSONS COVERED

Directive 79/7/EEC applies to the working population (including self-employed persons, workers and self-employed persons whose activity is interrupted by illness, accident or involuntary unemployment, and persons seeking employment), as well as to retired or invalid workers and self-employed persons.

Directive 86/378/EEC applies to members of the working population (including self-employed persons, persons whose activity is interrupted by illness, maternity, accident or involuntary unemployment and persons seeking employment), as well as to retired and disabled workers.

In Denmark, parental leave benefit, sickness benefit, provisions on accidents at work and unemployment benefits apply almost exclusively to the working population. Other parts of the social security legislation, such as old-age pension and invalidity pension, cover the whole population, irrespective of labour market participation.

Social assistance is available to the whole population.

5.1.5 UNEMPLOYMENT

The Unemployment Benefits Act makes it optional for employees whether to join the unemployment benefit scheme by being members of an unemployment fund. In practice most unemployment funds are closely linked to trade unions so that their coverage follows the organizational criteria in the trade union movement. Membership of an unemployment fund is open to full-time workers who work at least 30 hours per week and, if the fund in question provides for it, also for part-time workers who work at least 15 hours per week. Persons who work less than 15 hours per week are thus totally excluded from unemployment insurance; and persons with 15 to 29 hours' work a week have access to it only if the relevant unemployment fund is open to part-timers.

This treatment of part-time workers is perhaps inconsistent with Directive 79/7/EEC, as interpreted in the *Ruzius-Wilbrink* case. According to art. 4(1) of the directive, the principle of equal treatment implies that there shall be no discrimination on grounds of sex, either directly or indirectly, as regards the scope of the schemes and the conditions of access to them. It follows from art. 6(2) of Directive 86/378/EEC that where the granting of benefits within the scope of the directive is left to the discretion of the scheme's management bodies, the latter must take account of the principle of equal treatment. The same must apply to the Danish unemployment funds in exercising their right to decide whether or not to give access to part-time workers.

5.2 SOCIAL SECURITY DIRECTIVES AND OTHER LEGISLATION

There have been no Danish cases on social security issues under art. 119 of the EEC Treaty, Directive 75/117/EEC, Directive 76/207/EEC, Directive 86/613/EEC or the social security Directives (79/7/EEC and 86/378/EEC).

5.3 PROBLEMATIC CONCEPTS

Concepts like breadwinner, sole breadwinner, head of household, cohabitant, person living alone, and dependant do not give rise to particular problems in Denmark.

5.4 EXCEPTIONS

The principle of equal treatment is, according to art. 4(2) of Directive 79/7/EEC, without prejudice to provisions relating to the protection of women by reason of maternity. In Denmark, women are entitled to longer pregnancy and maternity leave with benefit than the paternity/parental leave with benefit to which men are entitled.

5.4.1 RETIREMENT AGE

Directive 79/7/EEC does not prejudice the right of Member States to exclude from its scope the determination of pensionable age for the purposes of granting old-age and retirement pensions, as well as the possible consequences thereof for other benefits. Denmark has made no use of this possibility; the retirement age has been the same for men and women since 1 January 1984. Prior to that date single women aged between 62 and 67 had the right to an old-age pension, whereas married women and men only obtained that right from the age of 67. As from 1 January 1984 everyone has been entitled to an old-age pension from the age of 67; no entitlement exists before that age.

Following the judgments of the ECJ in *Rinner-Kühn*[1] and *Ruzius-Wilbrink*,[2] one could question the compatibility of the Labour Market Supplementary Pensions Act, which gives only part-time workers with at least 10 hours work per week access to its benefits, with art. 4 of Directive 79/7/EEC, which is directly effective.

It is also lawful under Directive 79/7/EEC to discriminate on grounds of sex in giving advantages in respect of old-age pension schemes to persons who have brought up children; in the acquisition of benefit entitlements following periods of interruption of employment due to the bringing up of children; in the granting of old-age or invalidity benefit entitlements by virtue of the derived entitlements of a wife; in the granting of increases of long-term invalidity, old-age, occupational accident and disease benefits for a dependent wife; and in the consequences of the exercise, before the adoption of this directive, of a right of option not to acquire rights or incur obligations under a statutory scheme. Denmark has made no use of these options.

5.4.2 SEX AS A DETERMINING FACTOR

Sex is not a determining factor under Danish social security law, except as regards parental leave and benefit.

5.5 LEVELLING UP/DOWN

There is nothing to report under this heading in Danish law.

5.6 PART-TIME WORK

Following the judgments of the ECJ in *Rinner-Kühn*[3] and *Ruzius-Wilbrink*,[4] one could question the compatibility of the Labour Market Supplementary Pensions Act and the Unemployment Benefits Act, which give only limited rights to part-time workers, with art. 4 of Directive 79/7/EEC, which is directly effective.

1 Case 171/88, [1989] ECR 2743 (ECJ).

2 Case C-102/88, [1989] ECR 4311 (ECJ).

3 Case 171/88, [1989] ECR 2743 (ECJ).

4 Case C-102/88, [1989] ECR 4311 (ECJ).

6. ENFORCEMENT OF THE PRINCIPLE

The Equal Pay Act and the Equal Treatment Act are designed as individual employment laws. An individual who believes that she has suffered discrimination can bring proceedings before a civil court in accordance with the normal rules of civil procedure. If equal pay or equal treatment is guaranteed by collective agreement, the industrial procedure outlined in §1.1.1 above applies.

According to art. 2 of Directive 75/117/EEC, Member States shall introduce into their national legal systems such measures as are necessary to enable all employees who consider themselves wronged by failure to apply the principle of equal pay to pursue their claims by judicial process after possible recourse to other competent authorities. Article 6 of Directive 76/207/EEC contains a similar provision providing for the introduction of legal means of redress where an employee considers him/herself wronged by an employer's failure to apply the equal treatment principle.

The judicial process within the meaning of art. 2 of Directive 75/117/EEC and art. 6 of Directive 76/207/EEC must be interpreted within the context of art. 6 of the European Convention on Human Rights, by which all Member States of the EC are bound. This article provides that in the determination of his civil rights and obligations everyone is entitled to a fair and public hearing within a reasonable time by an independent and impartial tribunal established by law.

Industrial arbitration in Denmark is governed by the procedural rules agreed by the parties in a collective agreement. The hearing and the arbitration award usually are not public. One can query whether Denmark fulfils its obligation under the directives in leaving equal pay cases to be handled by industrial arbitration.[1]

Article 6 of Directive 75/117/EEC provides that Member States shall, in accordance with their national circumstances and legal systems, take the necessary measures to ensure that the principle of equal pay is applied. They shall see that effective means are available to take care that this principle is observed. The Commission had proposed a stronger provision, requiring administrative monitoring of the observance of the equal pay principle, but this proposal met with political opposition, in particular from Denmark and the United Kingdom.

---

1 See R. NIELSEN, *EF-arbejdsret*, Copenhagen, 1992, pp 45-48.

In the report on the implementation of Directive 75/117/EEC,[1] Denmark stated that under Danish custom the labour market organizations themselves monitored the implementation of collective agreements, and to a certain extent monitored their implementation in the case of employees who were not trade union members. It added that the Equal Status Council (*Ligestillingsrådet*) kept under review the principle of equal pay, but there would be no State control as such in Denmark in view of the fact that it would be contrary to Danish practice and the national legal system.

6.1 COURT OR TRIBUNAL PROCEDURE

6.1.1 ACQUIRING THE EVIDENCE

There are no special provisions on how to acquire the evidence in equality cases. Normal procedural rules apply. No forms are prescribed. A Danish employer has no obligation to furnish relevant evidence. As a rule the plaintiff (in equality cases the employee or a trade union) must do this. It does, however, follow from normal procedural rules that the party who is in possession of relevant material can be asked to put it at the other party's disposal.

There are no specific rules in Denmark about the provision of annual information to the works council on equality matters. Anything may be agreed by collective agreement.

Danish employers have no duty to provide trade unions with information for bargaining purposes.

6.1.2 BURDEN OF PROOF

By the amendment of the Equal Treatment Act in 1989[2] an explicit provision was put into the Act providing for the reversal of the burden of proof in case of unlawful dismissal during pregnancy or parental leave.[3] This was only a codification of what had already been established in case law.

In the minimum wage system, the collective agreement lays down the minimum wage. Most workers or employees receive increments based on a very wide variety of criteria. The general pattern is that male-dominated groups receive more additional payments than predominantly female groups, a fact which makes it likely that this wage system serves as a cover for indirect discrimination.

---

1 COM(78) 711, p. 27.

2 Act No 244 of 1989.

3 Section 16(4) of the Equal Treatment Act.

This is, however, difficult to prove. In Denmark, until EC law was invoked to change the interpretation of Danish law, the full burden of proof was on the employee's side. In an arbitration award of April 1985[1] in the *Danfoss-I* case, it was stated that the employees had not proved that the wage difference could not be due to reasons other than sex. Consequently the arbitrator found in favour of the employer. Where the burden of proof is placed on an employee in this way it may be impossible to discharge it in practice.

In *Danfoss-II*,[2] the Industrial Arbitration Tribunal referred questions concerning the burden of proof and the defences an employer might use to discharge this burden to the ECJ for a preliminary ruling under art. 177 of the EEC Treaty. The ECJ ruled that where an undertaking applies a pay system which is characterized by a total lack of transparency, the burden of proof is on the employer to show that his wage practice is not discriminatory where a female worker establishes, by comparison with a relatively large number of employees, that the average pay of female workers is lower than that of male workers.

6.1.3 COSTS

The main rule is that the loser must pay the costs.

6.1.4 LEGAL AID

There is a general legal aid system which applies also in discrimination cases.

6.1.5 REMEDIES

In employment cases the complainant may invoke all the remedies usually available in the law of contracts: for example, the court may declare the rights of the parties, the injured party may rescind the contract in the event of a fundamental breach of the contract, and the court may award damages for economic loss and, where there is special provision for this remedy also, compensation for non-economic loss such as injured feelings.

By virtue of the amendment to the Equal Treatment Act in 1989[3] an explicit provision was put into the Act providing for reinstatement in case of an unlawful dismissal during pregnancy or parental leave.[4]

---

1 Arbitration award of 16 April 1985 in the *Danfoss-I* case, published in *Arbejdsretligt Tidsskrift*, 1985, p. 197.

2 *Handels- og Kontorfunktionærernes Forbund i Danmark* v. *Dansk Arbejdsgiverforening for Danfoss*, Case 109/88, [1989] ECR 3199 (ECJ).

3 Act No 244 of 1989.

4 Section 16(4) of the Equal Treatment Act.

In practice the usual remedy in equal treatment cases is compensation at the level of two to three months' salary for violation of s. 2 of the Act on recruitment or s. 4 of the Act on dismissal (in practice most frequently on grounds of pregnancy). In addition, discriminatory advertisements, which are unlawful under s. 6 of the Equal Treatment Act, have given rise to a number of criminal cases in which the employers have been sentenced to pay minor fines (DKR 300-1,000).

In 1989, the maximum level of compensation for dismissal of an employee was raised from 26 weeks' pay to 39 weeks' pay,[1] and for dismissal on grounds of pregnancy or parental leave to 78 weeks' pay.[2]

In collective labour law there is a special sanction, the *bod*, which is an amount of money the Labour Court (*Arbejdsretten*) can sentence a party to a collective agreement (or members of that party) to pay to the other party in the event of breach of the collective agreement. If, for example, an employer violates his duty under a collective agreement to pay a woman equal pay, the trade union which is a party to that collective agreement, provided it is not a member of a larger organization, can bring the case before the Labour Court. The individual woman who is being discriminated against can do nothing. If the trade union is a member of a larger organization, such as the confederation of trade unions (LO), it is up to that organization to decide whether or not to raise the case.

If an equal pay case is brought before the Labour Court (which has not occurred so far) the court may impose a *bod* on the employer to be paid to the aggrieved party to the collective agreement, i.e. the trade union. If the woman who was discriminated against is a member of the trade union she can expect her union to pass on to her a sum of money to compensate for the under-payment. Collective agreements bind the employers to pay all employees (union members and non-union members) in accordance with the collective agreement. If in the above example the under-paid woman is not a trade union member, the employer has still violated a collective agreement duty owed to the trade union. The Labour Court will therefore impose a fine (*bod*) on him to be paid to the trade union. In this case the trade union will not pass on part of the money to the discriminated woman. She will therefore receive nothing even though a collective labour law sanction applies. It is a matter of dispute whether she is entitled to bring an individual case before the ordinary courts.

The courts may in principle award injunctions, or orders addressed to the defendant to do or not to do something, but in practice this sanction is rarely used in labour law. A court or tribunal cannot order the selection for employment of an applicant.

---

1 Section 15(2) of the Equal Treatment Act.

2 Section 16(2) and (3) of the Equal Treatment Act.

Article L. 152-1-1 of the French *Code du travail* empowers the judge to choose between using the ordinary sanction for violations of the prohibition of discrimination or imposing a duty on the employer to draw up an equality plan. There is no similar provision in Denmark.

6.1.6 CLASS ACTIONS

There is no class action system in Danish law. If a case is conducted by the trade union, this may in practice have the characteristics of a class action.

6.1.7 EXCLUSION OF JUDICIAL REDRESS

A Danish employer must observe the rules laid down by collective agreement, in relation both to individuals who are unionized and to individuals who are not members of the trade union which is a party to the collective agreement. A non-union member who is affected by the failure to apply a collective agreement has access to the ordinary civil courts for legal redress. There is, however, no individual access to industrial arbitration.

In matters where EC law is not involved, the general rule in Denmark is that a union member who has a right under a collective agreement must leave it to the union which is a party to that agreement to seek judicial enforcement of the right. If the union for one reason or another does not seek redress, the right is unenforceable.

It is therefore a difficult question as to whether a trade union member who is guaranteed equal pay in a collective agreement but whose trade union does not want to bring proceedings before an industrial arbitration tribunal can take the case to the ordinary courts; she cannot at any rate take the case to industrial arbitration, as only the parties to collective agreements can do that. According to s. 1 of the Equal Pay Act the Act does not apply when the right to equal pay arises out of a collective agreement. It may therefore be argued that an individual union member who considers herself damaged by the failure to apply the equal pay principle has no access to judicial enforcement in the event of her trade union disagreeing with her. This is inconsistent with EC law. It has therefore been argued that in this situation there must be access to the ordinary courts irrespective of the fact that this is in conflict with Danish tradition.[1]

6.2 COURTS AND TRIBUNALS

Conflicts arising out of individual employment contracts or concerning the interpretation of legislation governing such contracts are dealt with by the ordinary civil courts.

---

1 R. NIELSEN, *EF-arbejdsret*, Copenhagen, 1992, p. 44.

Denmark has, in contrast with most other Western countries, no special labour or employment courts or tribunals to handle cases concerning individual employment conflicts. No equality-specific enforcement machinery has been established. In collective labour law there is a Labour Court and industrial arbitration (see §1.1.1 above).

6.3 ENFORCEMENT AGENCY

6.3.1 TYPE

6.3.1.1 Labour inspectorate

The labour inspectorate has no special functions in equality matters. All public officials, including therefore the Directorate of Labour Inspection, are obliged to follow the Equality Directives according to ordinary administrative principles. This is to be done in such a way that, for example, environmental law and unemployment legislation should be administered in accordance with the principle of equal treatment, even though this cannot be deduced from the Equal Treatment Act. This principle has been explicitly applied to labour exchanges.[1]

6.3.1.2 Equal opportunities agency

The Equal Status Council was established administratively by the Prime Minister in 1975 on the recommendation of the Commission on the Status of Women in Society. The Council was confirmed by law on 12 April 1978 on the same date as the Equal Treatment Act was passed. The Equal Opportunities Act[2] has now replaced the Act on the Equal Status Council. The Council consists of a President, who is a Member of Parliament, and eight other members nominated as follows: one member each from the Federation of Danish Trade Unions, the Danish Employers' Confederation, and the Federation of Danish Civil Servants and Salaried Employees' Organizations (*Fællesrådet for Tjenestemands- og Funktionær-organisationer*); one member from the Danish Women's Society (*Dansk Kvindesamfund*); one member representing research into women's studies; and three members from the National Council of Women (*Danske Kvinders Nationalråd*). Appointments to the Council run for a term of four years. The Council is attached to the Prime Minister's Office.

6.3.2 FUNCTIONS

The Council's role is to promote the equal status of men and women in society, on the labour market, in education and training, and in the family.

1 In the Labour Ministry circular No 105 of 27 June 1978 on the Equal Treatment Act.

2 No 238 of 1988.

The terms of reference of the Council, laid down by the Prime Minister, specify the duties of the Council. One duty is to work as consultant as far as employment is concerned in cases in which exemptions from the Equal Treatment Act are required.

By virtue of the amendment to the Equal Treatment Act and the Equal Pay Act in 1989 a duty was imposed on employers and employees to give information to the Equal Status Council in discrimination cases. The Council was also empowered to grant positive action exemptions from the Equal Treatment Act.

6.3.3 REMEDIES

There is a criminal sanction in the form of a fine for violation of the obligation to disclose information to the Equal Status Council.[1]

6.4 COLLECTIVE AGREEMENTS

On the nature and role of collective agreements in Denmark, and their effect of equal pay and equal treatment, see previous passages in this volume, and in particular §§1.1.1 and 3.5.5.

6.5 CONTRACT COMPLIANCE

Contract compliance as a means of promoting equal opportunities in employment has not been used in Denmark.

1 Section 18 of the Equal Treatment Act and s. 5a of the Equal Pay Act.

SOURCES OF EQUALITY LAW

7. LEGISLATION

7.1 LEGISLATION IMPLEMENTING EC DIRECTIVES: EQUAL PAY

7.1.1 CONSOLIDATION ACT ON EQUAL PAY FOR MEN AND WOMEN [1]

Section 1

(1) No discrimination on grounds of sex as regards pay may take place in contravention of this Act.

(2) An employer shall give men and women equal pay, including equal pay conditions, for the same work or work given the same value.

(3) The evaluation of the value of the work shall take place on the basis of a general evaluation of relevant qualifications and other relevant factors.

(4) The provisions laid down in this Act shall not apply to the extent that a corresponding obligation to give equal pay arises out of a collective agreement.

Section 2

An employee whose pay is lower than that of others in contravention of section 1 of this Act shall have a claim to be paid the difference.

Section 3

(1) An employer shall not be allowed to dismiss an employee for having put forward a claim for equal pay, including equal pay conditions.

(2) It is incumbent on the employer to prove that a dismissal has not been effected in contravention of the rules laid down in subsection (1). However, this shall not apply if the dismissal takes place more than 1 year after the employee has put forward his claim for equal pay.

(3) A dismissal which has been carried out in contravention of the rules laid down in subsection (1) shall be set aside if a claim to this effect is made, unless it is, in special cases and after a balancing of the parties' interests, considered unreasonable to order that the employment relationship be maintained or restored. A dismissed employee may instead claim compensation. The compensation may not exceed 78 weeks' pay calculated on the basis of the average earnings of the dismissed employee, and shall be

---

1 *Lovbekendtgørelse nr. 639 af 1992 af lov om lige løn til mænd og kvinder*, Consolidation Act No 639 of 17 July 1992 ('Equal Pay Act'). This is an Act to consolidate the provisions on equal pay for men and women of Consolidation Act No 422 of 15 June 1989 with the amendments flowing from Act No 374 of 20 May 1992.

fixed with due regard to the employment period of the employee and other circumstances in the particular case.

Section 4

Section 3 shall also be applicable to sectors covered by collective agreements under which the employees are entitled to equal pay, including equal conditions, but which do not have rules on compensation for a dismissal which is not reasonably justified by circumstances of the employee or the enterprise. The claim shall be dealt with under the special procedures for settling industrial disputes.

Section 5

An employee may not waive his rights under this Act.

Section 5a

(1) The Equal Status Council may at its own initiative or on request investigate matters related to this Act.

(2) Employers and employees as well as their organizations shall on request give the Equal Status Council any information of importance to the activities of the Equal Status Council.

(3) The employer shall give any information required in order to make possible an evaluation of whether the provisions of the Act have been complied with. If such information deals with the pay conditions of individual persons, the persons concerned shall be given notice of the fact that such information has been given and that it will be treated confidentially.

Section 6

(1) An employee who believes that his employer does not fulfil his obligations to pay equal pay, including equal pay conditions, as prescribed by this Act may bring a case before the courts with a view to establishing the claim.

(2) If there is different treatment of men and women as regards pay, it is incumbent on the employer to show that the work in question is not of equal value.

Section 6a

(1) Violation of Section 5a(2) shall be punishable by a fine.

(2) If the violation has been committed by a company, a private company, a co-operative society or a similar body, the fine shall be imposed on the company etc. as such.

Section 7

The present Act may receive Royal Assent as soon as it has been adopted.

Section 8

This Act shall come into operation on 9 February 1976 and shall apply to pay relating to the period after the commencement of the Act.

Section 9

This Act shall not extend to the Faroe Islands.

7.2 LEGISLATION IMPLEMENTING EC DIRECTIVES: EQUAL TREATMENT

7.2.1 CONSOLIDATION ACT ON EQUAL TREATMENT OF MEN AND WOMEN AS REGARDS ACCESS TO EMPLOYMENT AND MATERNITY LEAVE ETC. [1]

Part 1

Section 1

(1) For the purpose of this Act equal treatment of men and women means that no discrimination may take place on the grounds of sex. This applies to both direct discrimination and indirect discrimination, in particular by reference to pregnancy or to marital or family status.

(2) The Act shall be without prejudice to provisions on protection of women, especially in connection with pregnancy or maternity, under Part 3 of the Act.

(3) The provisions of this Act shall not apply to the extent that a similar obligation to equal treatment arises out of a collective agreement, apart, however, from section 18(2).

---

1 *Lovbekendtgørelse nr. 686 af 1990 om ligebehandling af mænd og kvinder med hensyn til beskæftigelse og barselsorlov m.v.*, Consolidation Act No 686 of 11 October 1990 ('Equal Treatment Act'). This is an Act to consolidate the provisions of Act No 244 of 19 April 1989 on Equal Treatment of Men and Women as regards Access to Employment and Maternity Leave etc. with the amendments arising out of Act No 268 of 2 May 1990.

Part 2
Equal treatment of men and women

Section 2

An employer shall observe the principle of equal treatment of men and women in connection with recruitment, transfers and promotions.

Section 3

(1) An employer who employs men and women shall treat them equally as regards access to vocational guidance, vocational training, vocational continued training and retraining.

(2) The obligation to observe the principle of equal treatment shall also apply to any person who undertakes guidance and training activities as mentioned in subsection (1).

Section 4

An employer who employs men and women shall treat them equally as regards working conditions. This shall also apply in connection with dismissal.

Section 5

(1) The obligation to observe the principle of equal treatment shall also apply to any person who lays down provisions and makes decisions concerning access to activities based on self-employment. This shall also apply to the establishment, organization or extension of an enterprise and the taking-up or extension of any other form of self-employment, including the financing hereof.

(2) The obligation to observe the principle of equal treatment shall also apply to any person who lays down provisions and makes decisions concerning vocational training etc. and on the terms governing such activities.

Section 6

No advertisement may state that persons of a specific sex are wanted or preferred in connection with recruitment or vocational training etc.

Part 3
Pregnancy, maternity and adoption

Section 7

(1) A female employee shall be entitled to absence from work due to pregnancy and maternity from the date estimated to be four weeks before the birth. After the birth the parents are entitled to absence from work for a total period of 24 weeks, of which up to 10 weeks can be taken by the father after the 14th week following the birth. The right to absence may only be used by one parent at a time.

(2) The father of the child shall be entitled to absence for up to two weeks after the birth or reception of the child in the home or, under an agreement with the employer, within the first 14 weeks following the birth. This right is independent of the right to absence under subsection (1) above.

(3) If the child is hospitalized, the right to absence under subsection (2) may be postponed, see section 10(6).

Section 8

The time during which an employee has been absent under section 7 shall be included in connection with the calculation of seniority in the employment relationship. This provision shall not apply to pension questions.

Section 9

An employer may not dismiss an employee for having put forward a claim under the right to absence or for having been absent under section 7 or for any other reason related to pregnancy, maternity or adoption.

Section 10

(1) A female employee who uses her right to absence under section 7(1) shall within eight weeks following the birth inform her employer of the date on which she intends to resume work.

(2) A male employee who uses his right to absence in connection with the birth or reception of the child in the home under section 7(2) shall by giving notice of four weeks inform his employer of the date on which he expects the absence to start and of the duration of the absence.

(3) A male employee who uses his right to absence under section 7(1) shall not later than eight weeks following the birth inform the employer of the date of the commencement of the absence and of its duration.

(4) If the right to absence after the fourteenth week following the birth is shared between the parents so that the absence of the female employee falls in several periods, she shall in connection with the notice to the

employer under subsection (1) above inform the employer of the date of commencement and of the duration of later absences.

(5) In connection with absence under section 7(3) adoptive parents shall, if the duration and time of the leave have not been fixed when the child is received, observe the time limits laid down in subsections (1) to (4).

(6) A female employee who uses the right to absence under section 7(4) because the child is hospitalized within the first 24 weeks following the birth or reception in the home shall, without undue delay, inform her employer about the hospitalization. At the same time the male employee shall inform his employer hereof. The parents shall, without undue delay, inform their employers about the date on which the child is received in the home after the hospitalization. If the child is received before notice has been given under subsections (1) to (4), the time limits shall be extended with the time which the child has been hospitalized. If not, the notices given shall lapse and new notice must be given within two weeks following the reception.

(7) An employee who uses the right to absence under section 7(3) because the employee is subrogated to the other parent's entitlement to daily cash benefits shall, without undue delay, inform the employer hereof and of the duration of the absence.

Part 4
Void agreements etc.

Section 11

(1) Provisions laid down in agreements and in regulations etc. of undertakings which are in contravention of sections 2 to 5 shall be void. This shall also apply to rules etc. governing independent professions.

(2) Provisions in agreements and in the regulations etc. of enterprises which concern more than one employer shall also be void if they allow discrimination on the ground of sex in the fields mentioned in sections 2 to 4. This shall also apply to rules etc. governing independent professions.

Section 12

No deviation from the provisions laid down in this Act may take place to the detriment of the employee.

Part 5
Exemptions

Section 13

(1) Where the sex of a person is of decisive importance for the exercise of certain types of professional and educational or training activities, the Minister under whose competence the activities fall may grant

exemptions from the provisions laid down in sections 2 to 6, after having consulted the Minister for Labour and the Equal Status Council.

(2) The Equal Status Council may, after having consulted the Minister under whose competence the matter falls, permit measures which deviate from the provisions laid down in sections 2 to 6, with a view to promoting equal opportunities for men and women, mainly by redressing actual inequalities which have an impact upon the access to employment, vocational training etc.

(3) Permission under subsection (2) above is conditional on the approval of the representatives of the social partners in the Equal Status Council.

(4) The Minister for Labour may, at the recommendation of the Equal Status Council and after consultation with the Minister under whose competence the matter falls, decide that measures may be initiated in specific fields with a view to promoting equal opportunities for men and women without permission under subsection (2) above.

Part 6
Compensation etc.

Section 14

Persons whose rights are violated through non-compliance with sections 2 to 5 may be awarded compensation.

Section 15

(1) If an employee is dismissed for having put forward a claim for equal treatment under sections 2 to 4, the employer shall pay compensation.

(2) The amount of the compensation under subsection (1) above, which may not exceed 39 months' pay, shall be fixed taking into account the seniority of the employee and other circumstances of the case.

(3) Subsections (1) and (2) shall be similarly applicable where the obligation to observe the principle of equal treatment arises out of a collective agreement, but where the collective agreement does not give the person concerned a right to compensation in the case of a dismissal which is not reasonably justified by the conditions of the employee or the undertaking. The claim shall be dealt with under the special procedures set up for settlement of industrial disputes.

Section 16

(1) If an employee is dismissed in contravention of section 9, the dismissal shall be set aside if a claim to this effect is made, unless it is (in special cases and after a balancing of the parties' interests) considered unreasonable to claim for the employment relationship to be maintained or restored.

(2) If an employee is dismissed in contravention of section 9 and the dismissal is not set aside, the employer shall pay compensation.

(3) The amount of the compensation, which may not exceed 78 weeks' pay, shall be fixed taking into account the seniority of the employee and other circumstances of the case.

(4) If a dismissal takes place in connection with pregnancy, maternity or adoption, it shall be incumbent on the employer to prove that the dismissal was not based on these grounds.

Part 7
Miscellaneous provisions

Section 17

The Minister of Labour shall lay down special rules on the maternity leave etc. of seafarers.

Section 18

(1) The Equal Status Council may, at its own initiative or on request, investigate matters related to this Act.

(2) Employers and employees as well as their organizations shall on request give the Equal Status Council any information of importance to the activities of the Equal Status Council.

Part 8
Criminal sanctions

Section 19

(1) Violations of sections 2 to 6 and of section 18 (2) shall be punishable by a fine.

(2) If the violation has been committed by a company, a private company, a co-operative society or a similar body, the fine shall be imposed on the company etc. as such.

Part 9
Commencement

Section 20

(1) This Act shall come into operation on 1 May 1989.

(2) The Act on Equal Treatment of Men and Women as regards Employment etc., cf. Consolidation Act No 572 of 28 August 1986 and the Act on Maternity Leave etc., cf. Consolidation Act No 101 of 6 March 1987, are hereby repealed.

Section 21

This Act shall not extend to the Faroe Islands and to Greenland.

7.2.2 ACT ON EQUAL OPPORTUNITY BETWEEN MEN AND WOMEN IN CERTAIN EXECUTIVE POSITIONS IN THE PUBLIC ADMINISTRATION [1]

Section 1

(1) The authorities in public administration governed by an executive committee, a representative committee or by a similar collective management shall endeavour to have as balanced a composition of men and women as possible.

(2) On consultation with the Prime Minister, the minister concerned may lay down rules to the effect that subsection (1) above shall apply also to specific non-profit institutions, partnerships, private limited companies, and public limited companies which are not usually considered to be authorities in public administration. However, this shall apply only if the costs and expenditure of the activities of such non-profit institutions are mainly borne by public funds, or if the majority of the company is owned by the State or the company carries out activities according to concession or similar public authorization.

Section 2

(1) In cases where a board or committee etc. of the authorities and institutions mentioned in section 1 above is wholly or partly appointed by a Minister, those authorities and organizations which recommend a member to the committee shall suggest both a man and a woman. If several members are to be recommended, an equal number of men and women shall be suggested, and, in case of an uneven number, one more of one gender than of the other gender. The minister shall decide who shall be appointed as the member. Similar rules shall apply where authorities or organizations shall appoint members according to rules of law.

(2) Subsection (1) above shall not apply if members of the board are wholly or partly elected by direct voting.

Section 3

Where there are special reasons the authority or the organization may deviate from the rules under section 2(1). In such cases, the authority or the organization shall at the same time state its reason for such deviation.

---

1 *Lov nr. 427 af 1990 om ligestilling mellem mænd og kvinder ved besættelse af visse bestyrelsesposter i den statslige forvaltning*, Act No 427 of 1990.

Section 4

The Minister concerned shall report to the Prime Minister's Department every three years on the development within the scope of the ministry concerned.

Section 5

(1) This Act shall come into operation as from 1 July 1990.
(2) The reporting under section 4 above shall take place for the first time on 1 January 1994.

Section 6

This Act does not extend to the Faroe Islands and Greenland.

7.2.3 ACT ON EQUAL OPPORTUNITIES BETWEEN MEN AND WOMEN [1]

Section 1

(1) It shall be the object of this Act to promote equal opportunities between men and women in society.
(2) Within their areas, public authorities shall work for equal opportunities and may in connection herewith implement special measures in order to promote equal opportunities for men and women.

Section 2

(1) It shall be the object of the Equal Status Council to promote equal opportunities and the Council may on its own initiative or on request examine conditions relevant to the object of Act.
(2) The Equal Status Council shall give an opinion etc. under the Act on Equal Treatment of Men and Women in Relation to Employment and Parental Leave etc. and the Act on Equal Pay for Men and Women.
(3) The Equal Status Council shall decide whether an approach gives cause for any further investigation.
(4) On request, employers and employees and their organizations shall make any information available to the Equal Status Council which may be of significance to the activities of the Equal Status Council.
(5) Where the Equal Status Council is considering a concrete matter the Council may call in statements from specialists on the matter.
(6) Representatives of the Equal Status Council and the specialists mentioned in subsection (5) above may for the purpose of its consideration of

---

1 *Lov nr. 238 af 1988 med senere ændringer og ligestilling mellem mænd og kvinder*, Act No 238 of 20 April 1988.

concrete matters inspect the execution of the work in the enterprises concerned, if an agreement for such an inspection is made with the enterprise.

(7) The Prime Minister may assign other tasks to the Council.

Section 3

(1) The Equal Status Council shall consist of a chairman to be appointed by the Prime Minister and eight members to be appointed by the Prime Minister, so that

1 member is nominated by the Danish Federation of Trade Unions
1 member is nominated by the Danish Employers' Confederation
1 member is nominated by the Salaried Employees' and Civil Servants' Confederation
1 member is nominated by the Danish Women's Society
3 members are nominated by the National Council of Women in Denmark
1 member who represents the research on women shall be appointed on nomination by the other members of the Equal Status Council

The appointments shall apply for four years at a time.

(2) The Prime Minister shall lay down the rules of procedure for the Council.

Section 4

(1) A violation of section 2(4) shall be punishable by a fine.

(2) Where such a violation is committed by a public or private limited company, a cooperative society etc. the company or society as such shall be liable to punishment by a fine.

Section 5

(1) This Act shall come into force from 1 June 1988.

(2) Act No 164 of 12 April 1978 on the Danish Equal Status Council shall be repealed.

Section 6

(1) This Act does not extend to the Faroe Islands and Greenland.

(2) However, section 5(2) of this Act does apply to Greenland.

8. CASES

8.1 DECISIONS ON EQUAL PAY

8.1.1 ARBITRATION AWARD OF 8 DECEMBER 1977

FDB og LO for Kvindeligt Arbejderforbund i Danmark

In writing on 28 September 1977 the Danish Co-operative Society (FDB) and the Federation of Danish Trade Unions (LO) on behalf of the Danish Women Workers' Union (KAD) requested that I[1] make a statement about an equal pay problem, which could not be resolved under the collective bargaining procedures between FDB and KAD. An exchange of letters was debated and the disputed work inspected in Albertslund on 18 November 1977.

Based on the entry in the records dated 12 September 1977 and quoted below, I must give the following answer.

Following a succession of negotiations about the renewal of agreements between the parties dated 5 May 1975 concerning pay and conditions within the capital and outside, the following entry was drawn up between the parties on 12 September 1977:

> At a meeting on 12 September 1977 between, on one side, the Federation of Danish Trade Unions (LO) and the Danish Women Workers' Union (KAD), and on the other side the Danish Co-operative Society (FDB), there were negotiations about new agreements, referred to as 31.14.0 and 3.15.0, concerning KAD members employed by FDB. The main subject was whether KAD members employed by FDB in packing stations and central depots etc. can claim pay in line with members of the Danish General Workers' Union (SiD) employed in the same work places in accordance with the law on equal pay and the compromise proposal of 1973.
>
> No agreement was reached on this point. On account of this it was decided that collective bargaining should be resumed between KAD and FDB on the basis of the compromise proposal of April 1977 and that ... the question of equal pay should be resolved. This could be achieved by arbitration binding on both parties. The parties agreed to ask the County Administration Officer, Mr S. Wechselmann, to be the Arbitrator.

Following this the bargaining continued, and was concluded and entered into the records on 29 September 1977. These entries contain stipulations about basic pay; but according to the record entries of 12 September 1977, the question remains whether basic pay for members of KAD, employed at the FDB packing station at the central depot, should be the same as basic pay

---

1 Sigurd Wechselmann, arbitrator.

for members of SiD, employed in the same workplace. Agreement on basic pay was reached on 26 April 1977 between FDB and SiD.

On this basis the difference in basic wages on 29 August 1977 was as follows, in *øre* per hour:

	In the Capital	*In the Provinces*
SiD Agreement	2.069	1.735
KAD Agreement	1.862	1.654
Difference	207	81

It was agreed between the parties that the agreements for the capital and the provinces, apart from basic pay rates and certain bonus payments, were identical and covered identical functions regarding the disputed problem.

The work functions for which KAD had made a claim for equal pay is packing, done by 150 workers. This work is mainly done at the fruit and vegetable packing stations at FDB's central depots etc.

FDB has described this work as follows:

> A considerable amount of fruit and vegetables sold in the co-operative outlets throughout the country is delivered by the suppliers to FDB depots, unpacked in crates, sacks etc., and these goods are then packed into retail packing. The goods and the necessary packing material are brought to the tables in the packing area by store and warehouse workers, working under the SiD agreement. Workers under the KAD agreement then place the goods on the packing tables, where under a set division of labour the workers at each table do the packing, weighing and labelling (where this is not mechanized). Then the goods packed for retail are placed in boxes and put on pallets for transport by members under the KAD agreement.
>
> The pallets are transported by members of the Storemen and Packers' Union (LP) from the packing area to the loading bays in the central depot, from where dispatch to the shops takes place.
>
> The transport of goods to the storage hall in the central depot is carried out by members of LP. This is also the procedure in the transport of the goods packed for retail back to the storage hall from where the LP members do the dispatching and loading of lorries to the shops.

Work in the stores done by SiD members is described as follows:

> Receiving goods off lorries and railway wagons:
> The goods are unloaded from the wagons by fork-lift trucks, after which they are stacked by the fork-lift trucks. Where fruit and vegetables are concerned, it is important that they are taken from the wagons to the refrigeration storage. From there they are transported to the packing area and again from the packing area after packing to the dispatch areas. This work is done by so-called 'electric horses' (electric vehicles). In all 15 to 20 workers throughout the country are employed in this kind of work.

The dispatch work is the most important part of the LP members' work and is done by 'electric horses' and organized so that the dispatch worker can, from various listed computer data, select the goods for transport, load them on to pallets and check them off the computer data lists. The dispatch worker then drives the loaded pallets to the loading bay. From the loading bay the pallets are put on the lorries by fork-lift trucks and taken to the shops. A number of LP members furthermore work on returned empty packing materials (module boxes etc.), cleaning and storing these away.

To keep the record straight it is also mentioned that apart from the SiD and KAD members and foremen, some office staff (members of HK) work in the storage areas of the central depots; they have control functions as well as a certain responsibility for controlling the dispatch of whole consignments.

In relation to the sex distribution in the above-mentioned duties we are advised that women mainly work under the KAD agreements and that men generally work under the SiD agreements. It is, however, women who under the SiD agreement carry out the detailed distribution work, such as distribution of goods from FDB country stores to the individual shops. In exceptional circumstances women have been doing real dispatch work. In these circumstances pay has been in accordance with the SiD agreement covering this kind of work. In the rare cases where SiD members have carried out KAD work, payment has been made according to the SiD agreement in order to honour the individual's contract of employment. This interpretation of the works agreement has not been disputed by KAD.

At the inspection of the fruit and vegetable packing station at Albertslund it was noticed that women workers were relatively faster at work. The reason for this, it was explained, was that it was bonus work. It was also noticed that their work entailed a physical exertion, partly due to the working position and partly due to the placing of the loaded module boxes on the pallets. A similar exertion was not noticed in the male workers during their work as drivers and operators.

FDB has stated the following in support of its submission:

The compromise proposal dated 28 March 1973 provides in paragraph A1.1 that in agreements comprising women as well as men the agreed normal rates of pay are fixed ... at the same rate for both men and women.

The KAD agreement is for women only. The SiD agreement is not valid in the sphere of the KAD agreement.

Even though it may be argued that FDB on the basis of long practice was bound to follow the compromise proposal, no obligation can be placed on FDB to pay KAD members the same basic rate of pay as the rate set down in the SiD agreement.

The Equal Pay Act binds the employer to equal pay for equal work. There is no doubt that the workers under the KAD agreement did not carry out the same work as

> the workers under the SiD agreement. Therefore, there is no basis in law to meet the KAD demand.

However, FDB acknowledge the agreed opinion of the Employers' Federation and the LO that although the Equal Pay Act uses the phrase 'equal work', this must include 'work of equal value' as expressed in the EEC Directive, which forms the basis of the Equal Pay Act. But FDB dispute that work done by workers under the KAD agreement is of equal value to the work done by workers under the SiD agreement. FDB has commented as follows:

> When as here we talk about comparing work performances regulated by various agreements, the value of these performances must invariably be the price in *kroner* and *øre*, at which each separate work performance has been fixed during the negotiations of the individual agreements. Should deviations have to be made, a criterion for comparison must be established. It must then be up to the party wishing to deviate to establish these criteria and to prove the claim that there is work of equal value. Neither LO nor KAD, who have so wished, have established such criteria and thereby made an acceptable comparison.

When evaluating the importance of work in this case, it must be kept in mind that the pay for store and packing work at the central depot should be set for each group as an entity. There has been a tendency during the discussion to compare the packing work with transportation of packing materials and raw goods to the packing and transport areas. In total 15 to 20 LP members are employed in this work throughout the country; it therefore barely affects 4 per cent of the varied store work done by LP members.

During the negotiations the point of view has been taken by LO and the union that the value of work for various unskilled groups in an industry should be presumed to be equal. This is rejected by FDB, as it will lead to artificial and absurd consequences between the unskilled groups, as well as in relation to the skilled groups, which for various reasons do not receive pay rates as high as those who are making the equal pay claims.

LO and KAD maintained that the work done in the fruit and vegetable packing stations is a complete work process. The fact that it is covered by two separate agreements is because it is carried out by members of two different organizations. To state this as an argument against equal pay rather appears an evasion of the law. Both groups of workers are unskilled; there is no relevant difference in their training and qualifications, and in this case it is irrelevant that LP members in the affected place of work only do 4 per cent of the total work. The working conditions for the women workers are worse than the men's because of the physical exertion. It is the opinion of the labour side in the dispute that the reason for paying the women workers less than the rate agreed for SiD members is solely that women workers are traditionally paid less. Such sex discrimination contravenes the aims of the compromise proposal of 28 March 1973 as well as the Equal Pay Act of February 1976.

In the comments attached to the draft Equal Pay Act it is for instance stated:

> The words 'equal pay' in particular are interpreted so broadly in Denmark ... that an addition by the Directive to 'work to which equal value is attributed' barely implies any real widening of the scope for equal pay in Denmark.
>
> In the few instances where a job classification has been made for a task which is equal to others, it will quite naturally include the equal pay rules. Denmark therefore entered the reservation regarding acceptance of the Directive that — for reasons of clarity — in the proposed Danish legislation only the words 'equal pay' should be used.
>
> Both the Danish Employers' Confederation (*Dansk Arbejdsgiverforening*) and the LO referred to this when the Committee of Experts raised the question with the Government in 1977 whether 'equal pay for equal work' should be seen as a more limited concept than the phrase 'equal pay for work of equal value'.

During the debates in Parliament (*Folketing*) the Labour Market Committee wanted further explanation of this question. The answer by the Minister for Labour was as follows:

> The starting point for consideration as to which words should be used has been the desire to use the same wording as used in collective agreements, so that the rights guaranteed by legislation are the same as the words written into the collective agreements. By using the same words in both places it is assumed that no occasion will arise where the law may be interpreted differently from the agreements.

When the Directive furthermore use the words 'work to which equal value is attributed', despite the fact that art. 119 of the Treaty of Rome only mentions 'equal work', this must be seen in the light of the conditions in a few of the other Member States where examples of equal pay for 'equal' work only rarely apply to men and women with the same work functions.

The Commission wanted to prevent this kind of literal and crafty interpretation, which presumably Danish law courts would not adopt, ... through use of the mentioned phrases. In this way the individual jobs are given equal value regardless of whether they are done by men or by women.

Such formal and rigid systems are rarely used in Denmark and during the preparation of the Bill the parties in the labour market agreed that experience has shown that a wider introduction of such systems would not be desirable, as it would entail the risk of women being placed in lower grades.

Instead of operating with a job classification system the organizations were of the opinion that real equality can best be achieved through judicial interpretation of the words 'equal pay' as used in the agreements as well as in the law.

No classifications were made in this case.

The problem put to the arbitrator only concerns the question of equal pay in FDB fruit and vegetable packing stations etc.

Already the compromise proposal of 28 March 1973 restricts free pricing, creating certain pay difficulties between men and women. According to the preliminary work on the Equal Pay Act of 4 February 1976 the arbitrator finds it proper that the question in this case must be settled on the basis of a direct evaluation, independent of the usual wage pricing, of the work carried out by groups of workers in the disputed production process.

The work in the fruit and vegetable packing stations is carried out to prepare the goods for delivery to the FDB shops. It is carried out by two groups of unskilled workers. The work done by these two groups is found to be of equal value.

The arbitrator therefore finds that, in accordance with the Equal Pay Act, the same basic pay must be awarded to the KAD members as is paid to their colleagues under the SiD agreement.

8.1.2 ARBITRATION AWARD OF 29 APRIL 1987

Kvindeligt Arbejderforbund i Danmark (KAD)
mod Københavnske Grossisters Arbejdsgiverforening for Premier Is A/S

A dispute has arisen between the Danish Women Workers' Union (KAD) and Premier Is A/S as to whether the women workers employed by Premier Is do work of equal value to that of the men according to the Equal Pay Act.

The dispute has not been settled at an organization meeting and is therefore brought to arbitration with the under-signed judge for the Supreme Court, Erik Bjerregaard, as chairman and arbitrator.

KAD alleges that Premier Is A/S is under an obligation to its union member workers to make a payment of DKR 921,131.25 plus holiday pay at 12.5 per cent and pay for Sundays and national holidays at 3.5 per cent.

Premier Is A/S has submitted a claim for discharge, or failing that for payment of a lesser amount.

The facts of the case according to the information given are as follows:

Premier Is A/S is a member of the Copenhagen Chamber of Commerce. The women workers in the firm were remunerated according to an agreement between this employer's federation and KAD, while male employees were paid according to an agreement between the employers' federation and the

Union for Dairy Workers, a subsidiary branch of the Union for Special Workers in Denmark (SiD). The terms of these agreements are supplemented by resolutions from area negotiations directly between the firm and representatives of the respective groups of workers. The basic rates of pay per hour on 1 May 1983 were:

	Women	*Men*
Basic pay	21.42	35.41
Cost of living supplement	24.43	24.89
Special supplement	2.30	0.00
Piece work supplement	1.10	1.20
TOTAL (DKR)	49.25	61.50

	Women	*Men*
Basic pay	20.42	35.41
Cost of living supplement	24.43	24.89
Special supplement	7.55	5.20
Piece work supplement	2.65	1.70
TOTAL (DKR)	55.05	67.20

At the time of the extension of the agreement in the spring of 1985 the difference between the wages for the two groups had not significantly changed.

In a letter dated 15 July 1983 addressed to the Chamber of Commerce in Copenhagen, KAD informed the Chamber that the union's Glostrup branch had during wage negotiations with the firm repeatedly protested about the large difference in the basic pay between men and women — about DKR 15 — but had not succeeded in persuading the firm that this was clearly in breach of the Equal Pay Act, as both groups consisted of unskilled workers without experience in the production of ice-cream. The union requested in a letter that a meeting should be convened to solve the problem.

Such a meeting was arranged for 28 September 1983, but agreement was not reached and the union refused to commit itself. KAD then requested the Equal Status Council on 24 October 1984 to examine whether Premier Is A/S, by its different remuneration of unskilled women and men employed in the ice-cream production, had contravened [the Equal Pay Act]. On 9 November 1984 the Equal Status Council asked the firm to give an account of the difference in pay. In the reply dated 26 February 1985 Premier Is A/S stated among other things that the remuneration for the women workers in most cases, for example women workers employed for more than 52 weeks, was DKR 56.05 per hour in accordance with a local agreement between the firm and the union's Glostrup branch.

The women workers did the handling of packing materials, placed lids in dispensers, wafers in containers, sticks in the stick inserters and paper in the packing machines. They also packed the products in boxes, cartons etc. The male colleagues operated the machines which produce the ice-cream; they also did the mixing of ingredients, weight control, quality control according to set standards, and they recorded data about the production for accountancy purposes. The male workers were also responsible for cleaning and sterilizing the machines in the morning and evening and for cleaning the work areas. These cleaning processes require special training, which no women workers have received. These male workers had supervisory functions as production line leaders/team leaders in relation to the workers on their particular line; in other firms they might have been called foremen. They received a team leader supplement of DKR 8.60 per day, in accordance with the Dairy Workers' Union agreement. In the deep freeze and the cold store male workers did the palletting of cartons of ice-cream products as well as accountancy reports. For this work and for transporting by truck they received a special supplement in line with the agreement.

The reply finally contained the following information about the numbers of female and male workers:

	Women	*Men*
on 1 September 1984	12	16
on 1 December 1984	8	14
on 1 February 1985	14	14

In a letter dated 22 August 1985 addressed to Premier Is A/S, the Equal Status Council pointed out that the starting wage under the Dairy Workers' Union agreement was DKR 61.50 per hour and that the highest possible hourly rate for women according to KAD was DKR 59.35. The Equal Status Council requested the firm to give an explanation for the reason for these pay differences, together with a more detailed account of the actual work functions of the two groups on the production line and their conditions for carrying them out. If the difference in pay was, wholly or in part, a sign that the firm attached greater value to the men's effort in the production than to the women's work, the Equal Status Council requested an explanation for the reason for the evaluation.

Premier Is A/S replied to the Equal Status Council on 1 October 1985 that the reason for the difference in pay between women workers and dairy workers was that they were working under two different agreements. In order to decide which agreement to honour when fixing pay rates for women workers, it was necessary to consider whether they were qualified to discharge the special work functions covered by the dairy workers' union agreement. During local negotiations with KAD in the early summer of 1985 the firm had offered to start a training scheme which would qualify women workers to work as machine operators, but the suggestion had been dismissed.

As far as the description of work functions of the two groups was concerned, the firm referred to the letter of 26 February 1985.

In a letter dated 22 January 1986 addressed to Premier Is A/S the Equal Status Council requested further explanations about the training offered to the women workers, and the effect it would have on remuneration. The Equal Status Council also enquired whether the fact that the two groups were remunerated according to different agreements was in itself a good enough reason for Premier Is to apply the difference in pay.

On 14 February 1986 Premier Is replied that the firm was a member of the Danish Employers' Federation and was bound to honour the agreements. Both the dairy workers' union agreement and the KAD agreement are standard wage agreements, which in principle exclude payments not included in the text of the agreements. The two agreements are negotiated by two different unions, which in recent years have developed differently for tactical reasons, and through Government intervention and other conditions. The firm has followed the agreements without measuring the value of the effort by one group in comparison with the other. The firm did not consider it its duty to judge whether the pay differentials between the groups is sufficiently explained by the existence of two agreements. The differences in remuneration are not exactly desirable, but the firm has not been able to alter this situation, considering the agreement rules, association regulations and legal principles.

On 9 June 1986 the Equal Status Council replied to the enquiry made on 24 October 1984 by KAD. Having given a detailed account of the information produced at the hearing of the case, the Council pronounced its judgment:

> that the remuneration of the unskilled women who produce ice-cream for Premier Is contravenes s. 1 of the Equal Pay Act insofar as the firm does not pay the women workers at the same rate as the men irrespective of the fact that the work the women do in the production of ice-cream can be deemed to be of equal value to the corresponding work done by their male colleagues, and without there being any difference in the experience and training of the two groups which could warrant the difference in pay which exists.

The representative of the Danish Employers' Federation in the Equal Status Council requested that the question of whether it was a case of work of equal value should be decided by arbitration.

On 7 October 1986 KAD formulated its complaint for arbitration. The demand for back payment of DKR 921,131 is calculated for the period from 15 June 1983, the date on which KAD appealed to the Copenhagen Chamber of Commerce regarding the problem. The parties are in agreement concerning the amount, but the complainant maintains that the back pay should be from a later date. During the proceedings it was reported that Premier Is has suspended its production of ice-cream in Glostrup.

On 10 February 1975 the European Council of Ministers passed a Directive to implement the principle of equal pay for men and women. The Directive was implemented in Denmark by Act No 32 dated 4 February 1976, which provides for equal pay for men and women for equal work. By a judgment pronounced by the European Court of Justice on 30 January 1985, it was established that Denmark had not made all the necessary arrangements to carry out the Directive, as the Equal Pay Act did not enable employees in a sufficiently clear and precise manner to deduce that equal pay should be seen in a broad sense. The Court's verdict necessitated amendments to the Equal Pay Act, and these were passed by Act No 65 dated 19 February 1986.

The Equal Pay Act provides:

1. (1) No discrimination on grounds of sex as regards pay may take place in contravention of this Act.
(2) An employer shall give men and women equal pay, including equal pay conditions, for the same work or work given the same value.
(3) The provisions laid down in this Act shall not apply to the extent that a corresponding obligation to give equal pay arises out of a collective agreement.
2. An employee whose pay is lower than that of others in contravention of section 1 of this Act shall have a claim to be paid the difference.

...

5. An employee may not waive his rights under this Act.

During the debates in 1985 and 1986 on the proposed amendments to the Equal Pay Act, the Minister for Employment replied *inter alia* to questions put by members of the Parliamentary Labour Market Committee as follows:

- that the amendment did not alter the legal position, but merely clarified and defined the legal position,
- that not only should equal pay be given for identical work, but also for work which in spite of certain differences is of equal value to the employer, which is determined by the normal pay structure independent of a direct evaluation of the productive efforts by the respective groups of workers,
- that the Act does not hinder differences in remuneration for training, experience etc. which is important for production,
- that the character of the real work functions are included in the evaluation, whether it refers to equal work or to work of equal value, and
- that it does not excuse an employer from the demand for equal pay to refer to different agreements for different groups, but that the pay conditions for a group of wage earners according to a given agreement must be seen as an entity, so that no demand can be made that two different agreements are identical in every respect as far as remuneration is concerned.

The manager, Niels Rasmussen, has given evidence about the working conditions in the production department and gave the following information. One man and six to seven women worked at the wafer machine. The man was the team leader and among other tasks it was his duty to sterilize the machine, to mix the ingredients, start the machine, the freezer and the air compressor and to regulate the speed of the machine. He was responsible for the function of the entire line. He should either be a fully qualified dairyman or should have received a total of seven weeks' training at Dalum Technical School. None of the women workers at that machine had received such training, and they could therefore not deputize for him.

The machine producing containers with two litres of soft ice-cream was operated by a man. He had to have the same training as the team leader at the wafer machine and he received the team leader supplement. The machine was only operated a few hours daily and during the remaining working time he relieved his colleagues.

One man and between four to eight women worked at the machine producing one-litre cartons. The man was team leader and had to have the same training as the above-mentioned team leader, as his duties corresponded to the duties of the team leader at the wafer machine.

One man and six women worked at the machine known as RIA 2. The man was team leader like the above-mentioned other team leaders. A further two men worked at this machine for longer periods. Their tasks were placing and removing the moulds. This is a physically strenuous job, the moulds weighing 7.5 kg, and the women have shown no interest in taking over this work. The two men concerned were not required to have special training. They were remunerated in accordance with the dairy workers' agreement but received no team leader supplement.

One man and six to seven women worked at the machine known as RIA 1. The man was team leader and had to have the same training as the other team leaders, and his duties were the same too.

The manager, Niels Rasmussen, has further explained that if the firm, as happened on a few occasions, could not get trained team leaders, a man without any training would be employed. He would then be trained by the manager during a period of three weeks and would then operate under the responsibility of the manager. If a team leader was not present at his machine the women workers could call the manager, who had an office next to the production rooms.

The director, S. Bang Christiansen, has among other things explained that the manager was responsible for the production, and it was his duty to deputize for any missing team leader. The women workers had regular places at the machines but the team leaders did not. The cleaning of machinery and the premises was done with the aid of strong chemicals and, in accordance with the special training in dairy techniques, was therefore done by the team leaders.

KAD has claimed that the case is about whether the unskilled men and women workers who were employed in the production of ice-cream should have the same pay in accordance with the Equal Pay Act. This case is about the integrated efforts of both unskilled men and women workers who produce ice-cream products ready packed for delivery. The work which KAD members do in this process is of equal value for the production process to the work done by the men. The fact that some of the men have special team leader duties cannot warrant the difference in basic pay, as they receive a special team leader supplement for carrying out these tasks. Apart from this, the two men have for long periods worked at the RIA 2 machines and done unskilled work of the same nature and value as the work done by the women. Finally, KAD has referred to the statement by the Equal Status Council and to a settlement which the chairman of the National Conciliation Board reached on 8 December 1977 in a rather similar case. Back pay has been claimed from 15 July 1983, when the case was taken up with Copenhagen's Chamber of Commerce.

The respondent party has stated that according to the preliminary papers on the Equal Pay Act the decision on work of equal value must be reached on the basis of a genuine evaluation of the production efforts made by the respective groups. In this case the men and women workers do not carry out the same tasks, nor is their work of equal value. There is a big difference in their work tasks, and the men's work requires a special training which none of the women have received. The negotiations with KAD in 1983 were concluded without the question of equal pay having been raised, and this must be seen as a recognition that the case was not about work of equal value. It is of no importance that the basic wages under the two agreements are different, as the deciding fact according to the Act is the total wage. In support of their secondary declaration the respondents have stated that back pay ought not to be awarded right back to 15 July 1983, as KAD did not immediately after the organization meeting on 28 September 1983 pursue the case through the usual legal channels, but instead contacted the Equal Status Council, which does not deal with questions of equal pay. The firm has all along paid the wages in good faith under the collective agreements … .

No agreement and no majority vote has been reached on a settlement by the appointed members of the arbitration panel, and so it is for the arbitrator to make the decision, which is:

According to information produced during the hearing, the work carried out by the male team leaders was so different from the women's work, both in actual work and in responsibility, that there can be no question of equal work or work of equal value. The discrepancy in remuneration between the team leaders and the women workers does not contravene the Equal Pay Act.

But Premier Is has over a long period of time employed male workers at the machines in work which was equal to the women's work. Those male workers were, like the women, unskilled and did not require special training, nor did they have team leader duties. As in these cases it was a question of equal work, or at least work of equal value, the unequal remuneration of the male and female workers does contravene the provisions in the Equal Pay Act.

Taking into consideration that KAD left it for more than one year after the negotiations on 28 September 1983 before they took the case up with the Equal Status Council, the claim for back pay should be reduced to two-thirds, or the sum of DKR 614,087.50, plus a supplement of holiday pay and pay for Sundays and national holidays.

It is therefore pronounced thus:

The verdict:

The respondents Premier Is A/S must pay the employed members of the Women Workers' Union (KAD) in Denmark the sum of DKR 614,087.50 in back pay, plus additional holiday pay of 12.5 per cent and pay for Sundays and national holidays at 3.5 per cent.

Each party must pay its own legal costs and half the fees and costs of the arbitrator.

8.1.3 ARBITRATION AWARD OF 11 FEBRUARY 1985

Handels- og Kontorfunktionærernes Forbund i Danmark (HK) mod Dansk Arbejdsgiverforening/Danske Dagblades Forenings Forhandlingsorganisation for Vejle Amts Folkeblad

Between the claimants, *Handels- og Kontorfunktionærernes Forbund i Danmark* and the respondents *Dansk Arbejdsgiverforening/Danske Dagblades Forenings Forhandlingsorganisation* for *Vejle Amts Folkeblad*, a dispute has arisen about the remuneration of five female members of the union, employed by *Vejle Amts Folkeblad*.

As the dispute could not be settled by negotiations between the parties, it was brought to arbitration with a judge of the Supreme Court, Poul Høeg, as chairman and arbitrator.

According to information received, the facts of the case are as follows:

In the light of the technical developments in the use of display terminals, computers etc. within the graphical industry, a so-called 'screen agreement' was reached between, on the one side, *Dansk Typograf Forbund* (Printers' Union) and *Dansk Journalistforbund* (Journalists' Union), and on the other side, *Danske Dagblades Forenings Forhandlingsorganisation* (Negotiating Organization for Danish Daily Newspapers), about the use of data systems in the printing and distribution of daily and local newspapers, in which terminals are part of the working equipment.

In the preamble to the agreement (Part 1, s. 2) it is stated that the agreement extends, but does not replace, the existing valid agreements.

Part 1, ss 6-8 read as follows:

1.6. In cases where work functions cannot be separated and where several work functions are integrated in the workers' tasks, the agreement under which the workers are employed will normally apply.
1.7. Where the agreement involves a work function relevant to an area covered by another agreement, the present worker may continue working under the current agreement, but on new appointment the conditions of agreement must be altered.
1.8. At the same time as entering into this agreement it is necessary to give notice of cancellation.

In Part 4, which covers receiving, entering and coding of advertisements it is stated:

4.1. Entering all verbally received classified advertisements, including reactivating, stopping, correcting etc. is salaried work. Entering covers administrative data, typographical coding and format as well as the advertisement itself.
4.2. Entry on the terminal of all other advertisements is the work of typographers. The entry may include the administrative data which appear from the advertisement copy itself.
4.3. Receiving advertisements by telephone and composing manuscripts is salaried work.
4.4. Entering advertisements from paper manuscripts is typographical work.
4.5. Contact with customers and sale and receipt of advertisements is salaried work.

A minute entry, dated 8 October 1982, states that agreement was reached between the claimants and *Dansk Arbejdsgiverforening/Butiks- og Kontorvirksomhedernes Arbejdsgiverforening* that 'the national agreement between DA/BKA and HK will cover all administrative work and that HK therefore can only be part of the so-called screen-agreement with consent of DA/BKA, under the national agreement, paragraph 1'.

The union, attaching great importance to making 'the screen-agreement' a reality, declared:

- that the 'screen-agreement' is limited only to the production of daily and local newspapers;

- that the union will not during an agreement period use the 'screen-agreement' to implement other agreements, which would impinge upon the areas of the national agreements;
- that the union confirms that the 'screen-agreement' only concerns distribution of work tasks, without creating new monopolies.

Finally it has to be mentioned that the typographers' union's daily newspaper agreement of 1983 contains the following paragraph 28(4) concerning display terminals:

> For display terminals installed in advertising departments the following rules apply:
> (a) Operation of display terminals in connection with classified advertisements for which no actual manuscripts exist is carried out by those workers who previously received and prepared the advertisements in the advertising department.
> (b) Operation of display terminals in connection with classified advertisements for which actual manuscripts do exist, complicated advertisements and full-page advertisements are carried out by the typographical workforce.

Previously on *Vejle Amts Folkeblad* — presumably as on most daily newspapers — there had existed a sharp division between the administrative and the technical departments, but with the new technology, for example after the introduction of display terminals and computers, this division has become somewhat blurred. Before 1984 the union members in the advertising department at *Vejle Amts Folkeblad* received telephone orders for advertisements, wrote them down and handed them over to the technical department for printing.

At the time when the 'screen-agreement' was entered into, display terminals were not yet installed in the *Vejle Amts Folkeblad* advertising department. On 1 January 1984 they were installed and put to use.

Since that date five part-time female members of the union have entered advertisements directly on to the display terminals. The entry covers the text, certain typographical codes and format as well as administrative data.

The respondents have given the following information about the working conditions of these five workers, their weekly hours of work and the percentage of time estimated for receiving the advertisements by telephone and entering them on the display terminals:

Kirsten Lund Nielsen	34 hours	approx. 20-25 per cent
Tina Rasmussen	15 hours	approx. 50 per cent
Bentje Jeppesen	30 hours	approx. 75-80 per cent
Rita Madsen	20 hours	approx. 50 per cent
Sonja Berngard	30 hours	approx. 60 per cent

The rest of their working hours are spent on routine office work.

In a letter dated 24 July 1984 the claimants made the demand that the five members of the union should receive remuneration equal to day shift pay for typographers.

The demand was rejected and a meeting on the case was held on 9 August 1984. On the union's side it was stated that the five salaried staff workers and the typographers did work of equal value.

The employers did not see that the work was comparable, as there were entirely separate work problems for the two groups of workers. The minutes of the meeting also state:

> Concerning the conditions of the agreement, it was accepted that the work carried out by the salaried staff was covered by the national agreement between DA/BKA and HK, and that the work done by the typographers was covered by Danske Dagsblades Forenings Forhandlingsorganisation agreement with Dansk Typografforbund; see 'screen-agreement' dated 26 August 1982. Regarding the remuneration of the above-mentioned employees, it was made clear from the employer's side that this was based on the agreements and therefore did not constitute differential treatment.

As no settlement was reached, the claimants demanded that the case should go to arbitration. In the complaint, dated 16 November 1984, addressed to the Court of Arbitration, it was demanded that *Vejle Amts Folkeblad* be obliged to acknowledge that Kirsten Lund Nielsen, Tina Rasmussen, Bente Jeppesen, Rita Madsen and Sonja Berngard must be awarded the same pay as male typographers on the day shift rate. Alternatively, the claimants have limited their demand to those of the five, who in at least 50 per cent of the working hours are involved with entry of advertisements.

The respondents pleaded to have the case dismissed.

During the negotiations in the arbitration court on 8 January 1985, evidence was given by Bjarne Nielsen and senior shop steward John Fleborg for the union, marketing director Keld Petersen and manager Leif Christiansen for *Vejle Amts Folkeblad*. Bjarne Nielsen and John Fleborg explained the more technical side of producing advertisements on the display terminals.

Keld Petersen stated that the claimants' members also had to give advice to customers by telephone. Leif Christiansen said that the advertisements prepared by members of HK would amount to 2.5 per cent, or 5 per cent of the total. He also said that eight to nine female typographers worked in the composing room.

In support of their claim, the claimants stated that the work done by the five members noting and entering the verbally received advertisements, actually is the same — and obviously of the same value — as the work done by typographers on the day shift as far as written orders for advertisements are concerned.

Vejle Amts Folkeblad must therefore pay the union members in question the same wages as the above-mentioned typographers, according to s. 1 of Act No 32 of 4 February 1976 on Equal Pay for Men and Women, according to which every employer who employs men and women in the same place of work must give equal pay for equal work, if he is not already obliged to do so by a collective agreement. The Act was introduced to comply with an EEC Directive dated 10 February 1975, which amongst other things stipulates that there must be equal pay for 'equal work or work of equal value'.

The claimants also pointed out that it is already noted in the conciliation officer's compromise proposal of 1979 that the main organizations had agreed to find a solution to the equal pay problem, where this had not already been achieved, and that equal pay meant that equal pay must be given for work of equal value, regardless of sex. The compromise proposal of 1973 also stipulated that all restrictions on ground of sex on carrying out any kind of work were repealed by the implementation of the Equal Pay Act, and that work-related supplements must be fixed in the individual firms, regardless of sex. Furthermore, the claimants have referred to a statement issued jointly by DA, LO and FTF in December 1982, which says:

> Where as a result of collective agreements, to which the under-signed organizations are parties, there is an obligation to grant equal pay for equal work, it has always been and in our opinion always will be the case that the demand for equal pay also includes the claim for equal pay for equal work or work of equal value, just as in the EEC Directive and the ILO's Convention No 100.
>
> Consequently no dispute could arise between parties to such an agreement as to whether two work functions, quite dissimilar but of equal value, have to be regarded as the same work. Whether two work functions are of equal value has to be decided regardless of general pay settlements, on the basis of a direct evaluation of the efforts by the groups of workers in question.

Finally, the claimants referred to an arbitration award dated 8 December 1977 in a dispute between FDB and LO on behalf of the Women Workers' Union in Denmark. The dispute concerned the question whether KAD's unskilled members employed at the FDB packing stations at central depots etc., on the basis of the law on equality and on the compromise proposal of 1973, could claim remuneration in line with SiD's likewise unskilled members at the same place of work. During the hearing it was stressed by LO that both groups of workers were unskilled, and that no relevant difference existed in their training and qualifications. The arbitrator found for KAD and gave the following statement in the verdict:

> The compromise proposal dated 28 March 1973 already encroached on the free wage bargaining system, which dictated certain differences in pay between men and women. After the preamble of the Equal Pay Act of 4 February 1976 the arbitrators find it proper that the question in this case has to be settled on the basis of a direct evaluation of the efforts in the disputed production by the two groups regardless of the normal wage fixing.
>
> The job in the fruit and vegetable packing stations is to get the goods ready for delivery to the FDB shops. This work is done by two groups of unskilled workers.
>
> The work of these two groups is found to be of equal value to the production work. The arbitrator therefore finds that, according to the Equal Pay Act, the same basic pay must be awarded to workers under the KAD agreement as that paid to workers under the SiD agreement.

Consequently the claim — or at least the secondary claim — should be met.

The respondents replied that it is out of the question, on the basis of the Equal Pay Act in general, to switch from one agreement area to another as regards what is 'equal work' or 'work of equal value'.

The agreements are generally neutral in relation to sex, and naturally male and female workers receive the same pay according to each agreement. One exception, though, is KAD, an organization for unskilled female workers.

On the other hand, the HK agreement, like the typographers' agreement, is neutral in relation to sex, and it depends on the circumstances whether a place of work has male and female employees.

In addition to this, as for example in the case of the typographers, it is principally a case of minimum wage agreements for skilled workers, often with several years vocational training. This also rules out that wages paid to men and women according to one agreement be compared to wages agreed for men and women in another agreement.

The arbitration award cited by the claimants, the result of which the respondents accepted, was about normal wage agreements for unskilled workers, in addition to which one union specifically represented female employees. This case is therefore irrelevant to any decision in the present dispute.

Furthermore, there is no question of equal work. The five members of the clerical staff have performed, or may be required to perform, several other duties according to their clerical qualifications, just as the typographers have performed, or may be required to perform, other duties than operating the terminals according to their training.

Not even the 'common' or shared area of work, receiving advertisements and entering them on the terminals, is the same kind of work. This work, as far as the clerical staff is concerned, is inextricably integrated with the advisory sales promotion which they offer the customers.

Finally, meeting the claimants' demands would in reality lead to sex discrimination as it would entail that male clerical workers replacing any of the female clerical assistants would, owing to the difference in sex, receive less pay than the women.

The plea for dismissal of the case by the respondents should therefore be met.

As no agreement or a majority decision has been reached by the arbitrators appointed by the parties, the problem must be settled by the judge, who declares:

In deciding whether to give men and women equal pay for equal work or work of equal value, and comparing two groups with different training, it is not enough to stress the factual similarities between the work functions of the workers concerned. The wages paid, for example to a skilled typographer, are not only fixed according to his actual work, but are also related to what his vocational training enables him to do within his trade. Exactly the same applies to the clerical workers. Comparison of actual work functions between two trade groups, of which one or both are fully skilled, will therefore be irrelevant in deciding whether to give equal pay. In such cases it is necessary to view each agreement area separately, and it is not disputed that, according to the HK agreement for shop and office staff, the remuneration of men and women with the same or similar training should be equal for equal work.

The arbitration award of 8 December 1977, referred to by the claimants, is of no importance to the settlement in this case, as it concerns two groups of workers, both unskilled, and of which one group belongs to a union for mainly unskilled men, while the other union is almost exclusively for unskilled women.

As result of the above-mentioned facts, the plea for dismissal of the case by the respondents will be met.

Regarding the costs in the arbitration case, they will be awarded as stated below.

The verdict:

The respondents, *Dansk Arbejdsgiverforening/Danske Dagblades Forenings Forhandlingsorganisation* for *Vejle Amts Folkeblad*, are cleared of the claims against them, brought to arbitration by the claimants, *Handels- og Kontorfunktionærernes Forbund i Danmark*.

Each party bears is own costs and each pays half of the fees and expenses of the arbitrator.

8.1.4 ARBITRATION AWARD OF 16 APRIL 1985

Handels- og Kontorfunktionærernes Forbund i Danmark (HK) mod Dansk Arbejdsgiverforening for Danfoss A/S

A dispute has arisen between the claimants, *Handels- og Kontorfunktionærernes Forbund i Danmark*, and the respondents, *Dansk Arbejdsgiverforening* for Danfoss A/S, whether Danfoss A/S, by fixing remuneration for members of HK, is in breach of its obligations according to Act No 32 of 4 February 1976 on Equal Pay to give equal pay for equal work.

As the dispute could not be settled between the parties by negotiation, it was agreed that, although the dispute was not about actual interpretation of the agreement, it should be settled by arbitration with a judge of the Supreme Court, Poul Høeg, as chairman and arbitrator.

The facts of the case, according to information obtained, are as follows:

The conditions of employment of the clerical assistants employed by Danfoss A/S are covered by the national agreement of 9 March 1983 between *Dansk Arbejdsgiverforening*, *Butiks- og Kontorvirksomhedernes Arbejdsgiverforening* and *Handels- og Kontorfunktionærernes Forbund i Danmark*. This agreement — in itself sex neutral — is about minimum pay, and only determines minimum pay rates for workers included in the agreement. According to para. 8, productivity bonus systems may be introduced to replace or supplement the minimum pay rates. According to para. 9 it is regarded as normal practice that higher rates are paid, especially where skill produces more valuable work, or where more independent work and greater responsibility is required.

To facilitate a coherent rate fixing for approximately 3,200 salaried employees at Danfoss A/S, some 325 of whom are employed under the national agreement conditions, the firm applies a system of status-nomenclature to classify the various grades of employees in the firm.

In an explanatory account of the system it states *inter alia*:

Background and aims

Within industry, building and engineering, commerce and similar service trades, individual wage fixing is applied for almost all salaried staff members. It is characteristic of this form of wage fixing that no pay tariff binds the individual employee. The system implies that the rate for the individual employee is fixed in relation to the job tasks required, as well as to the skill with which it is carried out.

Individual wage fixing requires a system of splitting the employees into groups according to their work functions. For this purpose a system of classification of employees has been formulated (status-nomenclature).

The purpose of nomenclature is to facilitate an administration of positions of equal job value and of an equal degree of difficulty. It enables the firm to make fair comparisons of pay levels between various groups of employees, between firms and between departments etc. Status-nomenclature is therefore also an aid to wage statistics.

Status-nomenclature should not be used to fix wages for the individual employee. Wage fixing must take into account, apart from the work load, other factors such as the effort and skill required of the employee.

Fundamental concepts

The status-nomenclature is formulated on two fundamental concepts:

- the kind of work,
- the weighting of the work.

By 'kind of work' we mean a description of the activities, such as constructing, producing, buying, selling etc. By 'weighting of the work' we mean the total demands made for a specific task, such as knowledge and experience, creative efforts, leadership with responsibility for personnel and finance, nature and extent of contacts and variations in work patterns.

What is to be included?

Job evaluation must be based entirely on the work functions carried out by the employee in question. It is therefore the content and weighting of the task which must be used. *The way in which the employee performs the task, such as the effort and skill which he shows, must not influence the process.* More formal qualifications in training and length of service cannot influence it either.

The choice of job code must be made on the basis of the work functions which the job requires at the time. The task which the employee has performed or will perform must not have an influence. This means, for instance, that the tasks included in a specific job may be formulated in such a way that they deviate from the formal distribution of tasks, e.g. in relation to an organization plan.

As it appears from the description, remuneration is determined individually, but in such a way that, through certain objective criteria for the nature and weighting of the work, the employees are placed in one of 180 nomenclature numbers (wage frames). This status-nomenclature system contains in itself no more sex discrimination rules than the national agreement.

Following a dispute between HK and Danfoss A/S, an agreement was negotiated in September 1983 about which of the firm's status-nomenclatures in the future should be referred to HK-administration/HK agreement. Among these were nomenclatures No 2106 and No 4107, which will be mentioned in more detail later.

During the summer of 1984 HK found, during negotiations with the union's Sønderborg branch and the HK-club at Danfoss, that there were discrepancies between Danfoss' usage of the status-nomenclature system and the Equal Pay Act. The union therefore, in a letter of 17 August 1984, asked Dansk Arbejdsgiverforening to make a statement, or for a meeting.

Dansk Arbejdsgiverforening rejected this, by a letter of 27 September 1984, on the ground that in status-nomenclature systems and remuneration within the separate groups a pay differential based on the sexes did exist; it could therefore not be recognized that some of the differences pointed out by the union, in the average wages for men and women, were an expression of wage discrimination, as wage discrepancies between colleagues of the same sex as well as of different sexes solely rested on a fulfilment of the regulations laid down in the national agreement on remuneration of the individual employee.

They were, however, willing to negotiate the case and a meeting took place on 20 November 1984.

The minutes of the meeting recorded the standpoints of the parties as follows:

> It was the clear impression of HK that the system of job classification at Danfoss A/S fully described the nature of the work, its weighting and its task content, and for this reason the noted wage differentials between men and women in the same nomenclature is a breach of the compromise proposals of 1971 and 1973, as well as of the Equal Pay Act of 4 February 1976.
>
> From the employer's side it was maintained that the firm kept to both the compromise proposals of 1971 and 1973 as well as to the Equal Pay Act. Remuneration of HK employees at Danfoss A/S is, according to the rules of the national agreement, supplemented by a system of status-nomenclature, which is based roughly on the nature and rate of difficulty of the work. The employer's side therefore denied that sex-based discrimination in pay occurs by remuneration within separate groups in the wage-nomenclature-system. The employer's side also maintained that there was no concrete evidence of unequal treatment based on sex, as claimed by the union.

Agreement was not reached and the union, who reserved the right to pursue the case, lodged a complaint with the Court of Arbitration on 28 January 1985.

The respondents replied by a letter of 14 February 1985 and a meeting took place on 19 February 1985.

During this meeting the claimants made a final plea, that the respondents must acknowledge:

1. that the value of work carried out in the individual nomenclatures in the job classification system is the same, so that for work in the individual nomenclatures covered by the agreement there must be equal pay for men and women regardless of sex;
2. that the respondents are obliged to pay Eva Paulsen the same as John Pedersen, as both are placed in nomenclature No 2106;
3. that the indicted are obliged to pay Ingelise Clausen the same as Paul H. Knudsen, as both are placed in nomenclature No 4107.

The respondents asked for the case to be dismissed on the first point. On the second and third points, they reject these on principle, or alternatively plead for dismissal of the case.

The claimants have stated that point 1 means that the Equal Pay Act applies to wage fixing within the individual wage frame, but not in such a way that it excludes sex-neutral, individual wage fixing within the framework.

The parties have, furthermore, agreed that according to the Equal Pay Act no sex discrimination must take place when fixing the remuneration within the same nomenclature number (wage frame).

The claimants have in support of their claim particularly referred to a closer inspection of the fixing of the individual wages within No 2106 and 4107 in the nomenclature.

Nomenclature No 2106, in which laboratory technicians are placed, includes 16 union members (8 men and 8 women), as well as about 40 non-union members. The wage range is from DKR 10,500 to DKR 16,000 per month, and the pay for the 16 members has been fixed as follows:

x	F	DKR 11,225	
	M	DKR 11,742	
	M	DKR 12,000	
x	F	DKR 12,057	Eva D. Paulsen
x	F	DKR 12,070	
x	F	DKR 12,358	
	M	DKR 12,500	
x	F	DKR 12,858	
x	M	DKR 12,941	John Pedersen
	F	DKR 13,344	
	F	DKR 13,698	
	M	DKR 13,799	
	M	DKR 13,800	

M DKR 13,961
F DKR 14,101
M DKR 14,983

Those marked x are employed in the same laboratory, the rest work in another laboratory.

The average pay for the 16 persons is DKR 12,965, with the average pay for men at 13,215 DKR and for women DKR 12,713.

The claimants point out that Eva Paulsen (28 years old) and John Pedersen (30 years old) are both qualified laboratory technicians. They work at the same apparatus, so it is determined by chance which one of them gets to do the development work sent to the department. Apart from this work John Pedersen also works at a stationary apparatus in the laboratory, measuring atom-absorption-specteophotometry; but a similar apparatus is operated by Eva Paulsen at various places outside the laboratory.

Therefore it must be in breach of the Equal Pay Act that they receive different salaries.

Nomenclature No 4107, which concerns registration and dispatch work in the stores, included 11 union members (4 men and 7 women).

The wage frame is from DKR 9,400 to DKR 12,500 per month and the wages for the 11 members of the union are fixed as follows:

F	DKR 10,024	
F	DKR 10,275	Ingelise Clausen
F	DKR 10,578	
M	DKR 10,700	Poul H. Knudsen
F	DKR 10,706	
F	DKR 10,707	
F	DKR 10,725	
M	DKR 10,788	
M	DKR 11,084	
M	DKR 11,182	
F	DKR 11,282	

The average wage for the 11 persons is DKR 10,732, with the average pay for men at DKR 10,939 and for women DKR 10,614.

The claimants have stated that Poul H. Knudsen, who was employed in the stores under nomenclature No 4107 until 1 January 1985, is 36 years old and has been employed in the firm for five years. Ingelise Clausen is 35 years old and has 12 years service in the firm. Until 1 January 1985 they were both doing registration and making out orders for repairs, dealing with crediting and registering dispatch notes. It could be said that Ingelise Clausen in the mornings does the same work as the man who is paid DKR 11,084 per month and in the afternoons as the woman who receives DKR 11,282 per month.

The claimants point out that the given examples show that Danfoss A/S, possibly unwittingly, have been committing sex discrimination in wage fixing within the nomenclature numbers, where the various work tasks must be comparable. Here the individual differences in pay have to be for a good reason, and that is not possible in the above-mentioned examples, where the persons mentioned in the claim in pairs have on the whole been doing the same work.

The respondents have in response to this claim maintained that Danfoss A/S did not wittingly or otherwise discriminate between the sexes in wage fixing within the wage frame. The fixing is done after a long succession of objective and subjective considerations as to the actual nature of the work — which even within the same nomenclature may vary considerably — the respective ages, training and seniority as well as, more subjectively, but not of less importance, of the employee's efforts regarding responsibility, care, attention and ability.

It is entirely such factual conditions which have influenced the individual wage fixing. This has meant that the above-mentioned salaries are different for each of the employees, men or women, according to the individual's effort and skills and the detailed job functions.

The individual employees mentioned by the claimants do not have the same work functions: for example, John Pedersen has several more work tasks than Eva D. Paulsen, and an individual, factual evaluation has not shown that they should receive equal pay.

With regard to the plea for dismissal, the respondents have pointed out that it was ruled in the arbitration award of 9 March 1984, that as far as individual supplements under the national agreement were concerned, only the question of 'disparities', and definitely not adjustments to the individual's personal supplement, should be brought to arbitration.

As no agreement, or majority decision, was reached by the arbitrators appointed by the parties, this case will be settled by the judge, who declares:

Remuneration of the employees under the national agreement has to be fixed individually — as the claimants also acknowledge — within the individual wage frames, according to the principles of para. 9 in the national agreement, and with regard to the conditions mentioned by the respondents. This will lead to variations in individual remuneration (men and women), which is also the case at present, and all groupings, according to sex and other criteria, can expect some differences in average pay, especially within small groups (in this case, 11 and 16 persons).

Under these circumstances the claimant has to prove, in order to substantiate that discrimination has taken place, that the correct wage fixing is tilted against the women, and that it cannot be explained as a chance effect of the individual wage fixing, under the correct legal guidelines.

Such proof has not been brought by the claimants, as it has not been substantiated that the mentioned differences in nomenclature numbers 2106 and 4107 can be explained as chance effects of the individual wage fixing, according to guidelines referred to by the respondents.

At this point it must be stressed that the personnel material is very sparse. No 2106 only comprises 16 persons, although the information was that more than 50 persons had been placed in this group. No 4107 only comprises 11 persons.

In such small groups calculating average figures is of little use as proof material. In this connection it must be mentioned that according to information received, the 16 persons in No 2106 were working in two laboratories. In the first were six out of the 16 (John Pedersen and five women, among them Eva Paulsen). The other 10 persons were in the other laboratory (seven men and three women). In the first laboratory the average salary for women was DKR 12,113 against John Pedersen's DKR 12,941. In the second laboratory the average salary for the three women was DKR 13,714 and for the seven men DKR 13,225. No further information has been given about differences in the nature of work in the two laboratories, but the difference in pay in the two laboratories could *possibly* indicate that the work in the second laboratory is of a more qualified kind.

It is in the opinion of the judge very difficult in the area of minimum pay, by calculating averages based on so little material, to substantiate that the difference in individual supplements is caused by sex discrimination.

A possible indication may be found by considering the likelihood that the inequality suffered by the women would be at least as great by using a completely random distribution of the salaries in the two groups of almost equal size (8-8 in No 2106 and 7-4 in No 4107).

In the way in which the claims have been understood by the parties, the plea for dismissal of the case by the respondents must be accepted, and there is no special reason to refuse the second and third point in the claim.

The arbitrator wishes to note that if sex discrimination had been proved, it would presumably only be possible to recommend in the verdict that a re-evaluation of the wage fixing should be undertaken to remove the discrimination, whereas it would hardly be possible in the verdict to fix a concrete salary scale.

The costs in the case will be awarded as stated below.

The verdict

The respondents, *Dansk Arbejdsgiverforening* for Danfoss A/S, are acquitted in the case brought by the claimants, *Handels- og Kontorfunktionærernes Forbund i Danmark.*

Each party has to pay its own costs in the case, while the fees to the arbitrator and his expenses are to be met, half by each party.

8.1.5 ADMIRALTY AND COMMERCIAL COURT (*SØ- OG HANDELSRET*), 8 JULY 1987

Handels- og Kontorfunktionærernes Forbund i Danmark for Lilly Margrethe Nielsen mod KODA[1]

The task in this case is to decide whether the defendant, KODA, by paying Lilly Margrethe Nielsen (hereafter called the plaintiff) a lower remuneration than two other male consultants with the defendant, has breached s. 1 of [the Equal Pay Act].

The defendant, whose main business is to look after its members' performance rights according to the law on copyrights, has the exclusive rights to issue permissions to perform copyright music and/or texts, and to collect the royalties.

The plaintiff entered employment on 1 April 1977 with the defendant. According to the contract, dated 15 March 1977, the plaintiff's work would involve visiting certain music customers and advising them regarding calculation of royalties and filling in forms, partly at the request of the customers and partly at the request of KODA colleagues.

The plaintiff worked part-time for 4 days per week. The salary at the time of appointment was DKR 5,017 per month. The plaintiff made ad hoc visits to restaurants and commercial premises on Zealand, Lolland, Falster and Bornholm. She also travelled to Jutland for a visit in 1983. When she was appointed, a retired policeman was engaged at the same time as controller in Jutland.

---

1 Case F 43-1986; the case is under appeal to the Supreme Court.

At the end of 1983 the defendant placed an advertisement in the daily press, seeking to engage two consultants. The hours of work were 30 hours per week with varying working hours, and the districts were Central/South Jutland, Funen and Central/North Jutland. The job description was that the consultants should look after KODA's interests regarding the public use of music in restaurants, shops and shopping centres, etc.

The defendant subsequently, on 1 January 1984, engaged two male consultants. On appointment both were presented with the following job description:

> Duties (areas of responsibility).
> Consultation work:
> (a) Central/North Jutland and the Islands
> (b) Central/South Jutland
> (c) Sjælland, Lolland-Falster and the Islands.
> In cooperation with the next superiors and contact persons in KODA to register users of music by control visits and canvassing.
> Primarily: restaurants, commercial and retail premises (fashion, hair-dressing, shopping centres, health and beauty centres, etc.).
> Secondarily: music for work, tourist coaches, town fêtes, libraries, cultural centres, assembly rooms, local newspaper orders, etc.
> Inform about the KODA enterprise: verbal information as well as distribution of leaflets, tariffs, etc.
> Visit licensing authorities and give information about KODA according to the Home Office's circular.
> Give advice about reporting of music to KODA.
> Prepare reports for consultation work.
> Planning and control: according to district division of the area (larger towns in street order), the tasks must be done in districts following instructions from the next superior — then in co-operation with contact persons.
> Daily reports of visits etc. to be written.
> Where use of music has been established a form must be filled in specifying the conditions regarding the music.
> Monthly transport account.
> Regular visits to KODA and possibly from KODA.
> The next superior: Jens Carlsen
> Contact persons: Preben Klarskov and Bo Petersen
> Hours of work: part-time (30 hours), variable working hours, possibly day, evening, Saturday, Sunday.
> Requirements: telephone and car.

Shortly afterwards the plaintiff also received a job description.

During the autumn the plaintiff learned that the male consultants received higher salaries than she did. Her salary was DKR 9,642 per month, while that of the male consultants was DKR 11,334 with bonus supplements in relation to the value of contracts entered into. The plaintiff wrote to the defendant concerning this. She received a written reply on 29 November 1984, which said:

> ... In your letter you also mention the question of salary, as you have learned that your colleagues earn approximately 33 per cent more than you do. In this

> connection, I must point out that everyone in KODA is paid individually according to qualifications, field of work, efforts, results, seniority, etc. Any difference in pay is due to weighing up of these factors and is therefore not due to error … .

The plaintiff commented on this letter in writing on 6 December 1984, but the defendant did not alter his opinion, except that the plaintiff got a bonus arrangement.

The plaintiff then approached the Equal Status Council. Their reply letter of 25 January 1985 to the defendant raised the question of equal pay for the three consultants.

The defendant replied to the Equal Status Council by letter of 7 March 1984.[1] In it we find *inter alia*:

> … From 1 January 1984 it was decided to employ two consultants, who in addition to the previous control functions in connection with the use of music in restaurants, commercial and retail premises, should look after a series of duties of an informative and investigative nature. To illustrate this: contacting the licensing authorities; contacting public institutions, including libraries; canvassing all music-using groups; preparing information material and contributing to KODA's membership paper; canvassing in connection with reporting of music, including control of music repertoires; attending planning meetings concerning KODA's canvassing.
>
> Experience with our previous consultants/controllers, as well as the above-mentioned extension of responsibility areas/tasks meant that, in connection with the vacancy advertisement, we made a series of demands on the applicants for qualifications, which none of our previous consultants/controllers possessed, in our opinion. In this connection we must inform you that when we decided to employ two consultants in Jutland/Funen areas, we contemplated transferring, or possibly dismissing, Lilly Margrethe Nielsen, but considering her seniority we decided to let her continue her employment, though under stricter guidance. There has been no talk of extending Lilly Margrethe Nielsen's responsibilities/tasks, although we realize that a job description corresponding to the newly appointed consultants was mistakenly given to Lilly Margrethe Nielsen by a department leader in our sales department.

The plaintiff resigned her employment with KODA on 31 October 1985 for health reasons.

In this case, brought on 13 March 1986, the plaintiff, *Handels- og Kontorfunktionærernes Forbund i Danmark* representing Lilly Margrethe Nielsen, has claimed that the defendant KODA is bound to pay DKR 66,244 plus the usual interest from the commencement of the case, plus holiday pay for 1984 of DKR 4,631.65 and holiday pay for 1985 of DKR 3,648.90, or alternatively a lesser amount according to the judgment of the court.

The demand has been put together as follows:

Difference in pay 1.1 - 31.12.1984	DKR 19,818
Bonus 1984	DKR 17,235

---

1 The original Danish report gives this date as 1984, although in accordance with the sequence of events this may be a misprint.

Difference in pay 1.1 - 31.10.1985	DKR 17,158
Bonus 1.1 - 31.10.1985	DKR 12,033
TOTAL	DKR 66,244

The defendant pleads for dismissal of the case.

During the court procedure, evidence was given by the plaintiff, the director of the defendant Niels Bak, consultant Niels Peter Poulsen, consultant Jørgen Bo Larsen and sales manager Jens Carlsen.

The plaintiff explained that she had clerical training and has worked as a clerical assistant for four years, after which she taught as an English teacher at evening classes for eight years. She has also been a course secretary and a secretary, translator and bookkeeper in a larger business. She was recommended to the defendant by an employee at the time. At the interview, she presented her references from previous employments, but no mention was made of them. She has not since been asked to show them. At the appointment she was informed that she would be remunerated according to the national rules. Her work consisted of visiting shops and restaurants in Zealand, Lolland-Falster and Bornholm. On journeys to Lolland-Falster and Bornholm her hours of work varied. In the shops the work was partly to check and partly of an advisory nature. She did not visit libraries and larger places of work, as this was outside her field of work. On a couple of occasions she visited police stations for information whether a restaurant had a licence. She has been informed that a few complaints have been made against her, but she has never been criticized for it. In 1983 she suggested to the defendant that she could make a canvassing trip to Jutland, which was accepted by the defendant. She achieved a good result, but with no increase in pay. She thinks that the reason for employing two new consultants was her good result in 1983. She knew that two new consultants were to be employed, bud did not know the job descriptions. In February 1984 she was called to a meeting with the defendant, manager Ib Bo Larsen and sales manager Jens Carlsen. At the meeting she was introduced to the new system and was given the job description, which was examined. She was under the impression that she had to wait for the other consultants to get into the work, but she expected to have to carry out what was mentioned in the job description. She asked for a bonus arrangement at the meeting, but the defendant told her to use the title of consultant.

After 1 January 1984 her work became more centrally controlled. She was 'directed' from area to area, but the nature of the work did not change. She has only spoken to the other two consultants at two KODA events. On one of these occasions she was told that they had a bonus arrangement and, later, that they received higher salaries. During her employment her salary was regulated annually, but she had not been informed that the defendant had abandoned the use of the national rules.

At the beginning of January 1985 she had a meeting with director Niels Bak, who was then the office manager, Jens Carlsen and Ib Bo Larsen, at which her salary was discussed. The defendant offered her a bonus arrangement to re-adjust her salary as from 1 October 1985. She turned down the bonus arrangement in order not to miss the 'equal pay' rights. She was told that the other consultants visited libraries, which she also offered to do. She was not asked to undertake factory visits or to visit the Bella Centre. Not until the defendant's reply to the Equal Status Council did she learn that the defendant had considered dismissing her.

Director Niels Bak explained, that on 1 February 1983, he was appointed office manager and is now director of KODA. After his appointment, he was surprised by the stagnating income outside the area of Danish radio and TV, and he found it necessary to find more information about KODA's work, for example from the police and at libraries. He contemplated for a long time the possibility of improving efforts. At KODA it was known that Jutland was a rarely visited area, and the journey made by the plaintiff in 1983 had been proof of this. During a conversation with Jens Carlsen and Ib Bo Larsen he learned that they did not think that the plaintiff was open and creative and had sufficient initiative to carry out the new information tasks. It was contemplated dismissing the plaintiff, who had the largest district, Zealand, but as this is not the defendant's policy, it was decided to let the plaintiff continue until it was known how the new appointments would function. The requirement of the new consultants was that they have sales and planning experience. About 10 persons were asked to an interview, both men and women, in each district, and the new consultants were chosen because of their qualifications and personality. At the pay negotiations, their previous salaries were stated, after which the witness offered a salary which they could be expected to accept. As the defendant attached great importance to informative and other not directly remunerative tasks, a fixed salary was offered plus, as supplement, a bonus arrangement. Every employee now receives individual salaries related to their qualifications, just as seniority plays a certain role. The two new consultants still receive the same salaries, as there has been no reason for individual alterations. When appointing the plaintiff the predecessor of the witness used a so-called KODA wage-scale.

For geographical reasons the two new consultants cannot be directed as strictly as the plaintiff. These consultants negotiate independently on a rather high level, while the previous controllers only paid visits and pointed out the duty to pay KODA royalties. One of the consultants, Niels Peter Poulsen, got an agreement with Dansk Supermarked. Negotiations for this started in 1984. The witness did not think that the plaintiff was capable of such tasks, and it was not desirable for the plaintiff to enter the areas of information.

The job description, the first issued by the defendant, was formulated when it was decided to alter the duties of the controllers/consultants. The division of primary and secondary tasks depended entirely on how well the area was covered. The new consultants had only been with the firm a short time, when Jens Carlsen took them on a tour of visits to restaurants and shops. They started 'from the bottom' as the plaintiff had done, and the higher starting salary was an investment for the future. The consultants have always planned their own work, reporting when they started work in a district. The plaintiff, however, was given a map from head office, which planned her work. The firm considered the jobs of the plaintiff and the two new consultants as entirely different jobs.

At the meeting in January 1984 it was intended that the plaintiff was to be given the job description as a guideline only to the kind of work required of the other consultants. It was considered risky to give the plaintiff negotiation drafts on the same level as the other two, because of the previous complaints.

After her resignation her district has been divided up, and the alteration plans completed throughout the country.

Consultant Niels Peter Poulsen has explained that he was trained as a bookseller and a teacher. He was a teacher for ten years and chairman of the education council; he was also a salesman in the footwear business. Apart from this he is very interested in music. He applied for the job at KODA because the informative tasks appealed to him. During the interview prior to appointment with Niels Bak and Ib Bo Larsen the talk was about the field of work and qualifications, and he learned that the defendant was interested in re-planning the work. Not until later did he receive the job description in writing. He was offered a salary corresponding to three-quarters of that of a teacher with six to seven years' service, plus a bonus, which he accepted. Since then he has only received the usual increases and no other supplements. After a short introduction period Jens Carlsen came to Jutland to advise on the work in the shops and restaurants department. He has never received instructions for work planning. He has visited several mess rooms to contact the mess administrators, just as in 1985 he visited several tour operators. He has done a lot of investigative work of 'music while you work' in larger firms. This started in 1985 after an agreement with *Dansk Arbejdsgiverforening* (employers' organization), just as he has negotiated a separate contract with the supermarket. Of the more general information, work visits to libraries and attendance at the annual meeting of the Association of Danish Choirmasters must be mentioned. He also visits the police to obtain information and report on KODA. Since 1984 he has had contact with KODA members by going around the venues to check what is being played. He is out approximately one night a week. As consultant he has also taken part in the planning of leaflet materials. During 1984 approximately 90 per cent of his work was of an investigative and checking nature, but already in 1985 this changed to work of a more informative nature. Now he spends approximately 60 per cent of his time contacting the users and the rest on information work.

Every third month a consultant meeting was held with Jens Carlsen and Preben Klarskov, but the plaintiff did not take part. That was no surprise to him, as he thought the plaintiff had had previous training. At these meetings the latest developments and plans for the future were discussed. On a journey to Switzerland he spoke to the plaintiff about salaries and was surprised to hear that the plaintiff received a different amount.

Consultant Jørgen Bo Larsen has explained that he is commercially trained and has been employed in commercial and industrial firms, in insurance, as well as having been self-employed. He has also attended several adult education courses. During the interview with Niels Bak and Ib Bo Larsen the importance of self-discipline and independent work was stressed. The defendant mentioned that a special remuneration scale existed at KODA.

Following the appointment on 1 January 1984 he was introduced to the defendant in Copenhagen, and after that Jens Carlsen took him out to visit shops and restaurants. The job description, which he regarded as the basis of the work, was forwarded together with the letter of acceptance.

During the summer of 1984 he visited youth hostels, homes for seamen and airports, and visited libraries and police stations to obtain information. Later he has visited leisure and youth clubs. He has negotiated agreements about the use of music in tourist coaches. At the end of 1984 an agreement was reached between *Dansk Arbejdsgiverforening* and the defendant regarding 'music while you work', which meant quite a considerable amount of work to find the firms. He has visited about 150 of them. His hours of work vary and he does the planning himself. The defendant does not know which customers he visits on any day. The work has changed to a more informative nature.

He has taken part in consultant meetings in Copenhagen, but the plaintiff did not take part in these.

Since his appointment he has only received the normal salary increases. He has never mentioned pay and work conditions to the plaintiff.

Marketing Manager Jens Carlsen has explained that the reason for appointing the two new consultants was a decision taken by the new leadership in KODA to change the marketing. These new consultants should be outgoing, experienced in negotiation and flexible, and he did not think that the plaintiff had those qualifications. The witness did not take part in the interviews or in the pay discussion. The salaries were to be on a level between public and private rates for persons with the required qualifications,

.which was necessary in order to get suitable personnel. The job description was handed to the two consultants in January 1984 at the introduction meeting. Following this meeting they were sent out visiting restaurants and shops. Later the work was expanded to cover exhibitions/trade fairs and tourist coach operators in 1984/85. The plaintiff meanwhile had to continue her usual work.

The plaintiff did receive the job description but had to work with the primary groups, shops and restaurants, as the defendant did not think that she could manage the other tasks. Negotiations with larger firms, major users and licensing authorities were, for Zealand, done from head office. He was unaware of the plaintiff's previous employments, but thought after conversations with her and about her that he could judge her qualifications. He received several complaints from customers about the plaintiff not giving sufficiently good information. These complaints, when relevant, were passed on to the plaintiff. The plaintiff's work was tightly planned, giving her maps covering the areas she was to visit. She had previously visited these places. The change from controller to consultant only happened for marketing reasons. The two new consultants planned their own work. In 1984, 90 per cent of their work corresponded to the work of the plaintiff, while in 1985 this only applied to 70 per cent.

The lawyer for the plaintiff has pointed out that the defendant, by paying the plaintiff a lower salary than her two colleagues, is in breach of s. 1 of the Equal Pay Act. This Act obliges the employer to give equal pay for equal work or for work of equal value. According to the protection aims of this Act a distribution of the burden of proof must be made, so that the plaintiff must substantiate that the claim concerns equal work, and the defendant has to substantiate that no sex discrimination has taken place to affect the difference in remuneration. All three consultants received the job description, which must form the basis for the legal adjustment of the relationship between the consultants and the defendant. According to the job description, which in its use of words also applied to the plaintiff, no difference in work planning existed, and the abnormal working hours for the two new consultants were entirely due to their other functions. Furthermore, the work was the same for all of them in 1984, and in 1985 the majority of the work was the same. Not until the plaintiff raised the case were the supplementary tasks in the job description described as secondary tasks. These tasks are described by the other consultants as 'not difficult', and the plaintiff could easily have managed them. The defendant did not wish this, although the plaintiff had the same contractual duties as the other two consultants. These missing tasks must be regarded of no importance to the judgment of work value. The salary fixing was, according to the plaintiff's letter to the Equal Status Council, done individually, but this is not verified by statements from the consultants. Seniority has not carried any great importance either in view of the difference in salaries between the plaintiff and the other consultants. The work required no special vocational qualifications, and it can hardly have been of such great importance, as the plaintiff was never asked about her qualifications. Experience and achievement of results did not carry much weight either, as the two new consultants received higher salaries than the plaintiff from the day of their appointment. Neither did she have a bonus arrangement. Individual remuneration does not appear to apply either, as the two consultants still receive the same salary. None of the factors given by the defendant for variation in remuneration seem to have been applied, and as the plaintiff in 1984 has on the whole done the same work as the other two, she ought to receive the same pay.

The lawyer for the defendant has maintained that the difference in pay had no sex-related reasons, therefore the legal standard of the Act has not been breached. In the preamble to the Act a series of qualifications are mentioned, such as training, experience, responsibility, attention to care and the nature of work, which may contribute as factors in wage fixing. The burden of proof of sex discrimination in wage fixing must rest solely with the plaintiff, and she has failed to discharge it. From the letter to the Equal Status Council and from director Bak's statement, it appears that the plaintiff wanted to change her image from being a controller to being a consultant. Somewhere in the chain of this changed strategy it was desired to employ consultants, who were to work more independently and who could negotiate. They also had to be involved in planning, which they were at the quarterly meetings, in which the plaintiff did not take part. The defendant therefore had to estimate qualifications within areas different from those applying previously. The consultants' statements of previous employments and their personal appearances were the basis for their employment. When fixing the remuneration, which is individual, it was done with an eye to public pay as well as with regard to competitiveness. The qualifications of the two employees were considered equal. The qualifications of the plaintiff, it was thought, could be judged from her work so far, and on the basis of that, she was not regarded as suitable. She therefore had to continue her usual work, and it does not appear to be clear why she was given the job description. The new consultants were to carry out different tasks from the plaintiff, although they were initially doing the same work. According to the explanation, a gradual change in work has occurred, and although the qualifications were not immediately used to the full, it must be appropriate to take them into consideration for the fixing of salaries. The purpose of the appointments was the changed strategy, which required different qualifications, and to achieve this it was essential to pay a higher salary. These factors, and not sex discriminatory factors, were entirely the reason for the difference in pay, and therefore no breach has occurred of the equal pay principle.

Pronouncement of the Court:

Having heard the evidence it is established that the defendant in 1983 wished to change strategy in order to become more sales-oriented and informative, and that this was the reason for employing the two new consultants. In this connection the defendant must be entitled to make an assessment as to whether the plaintiff is suited to the new tasks, and the plaintiff has no claim to take part in this. According to the evidence the defendant did not wish to change the plaintiff's position. The fact that the title of the plaintiff's position was changed is found to be of no importance. The background to the handing out of the job description appears unclear, but as the duties in the plaintiff's district continued to be shared between the plaintiff and the head office, it is not substantiated that this was to affect the plaintiff.

When estimating whether the plaintiff's work was of equal value to the work of the others, it is stressed that only for a limited period was it almost identical, and that the other two consultants were given more independent tasks. The plaintiff's work and its purpose was therefore so different from the others that it warranted different pay. Accordingly we find for the defendant.

Costs awarded as stated below.

The verdict:

Defendant, KODA, is cleared of the claim brought by the plaintiff, *Handels- og Kontorfunktionærernes Forbund i Danmark*, representing Lilly Margrethe Nielsen.,

The plaintiff must pay DKR 11,000 costs to the defendant within 14 days of this verdict.

8.2 DECISIONS ON EQUAL TREATMENT

8.2.1 ADMIRALTY AND COMMERCIAL COURT IN COPENHAGEN, SHD, 11 OCTOBER 1979

Sømændenes Forbund i Danmark for Sonja J. Jensen mod Rederiet A.P. Møller[1]

A female able seaman, M, through a job centre, found work on a vessel belonging to the shipping company R, but was refused, as a result of a decision by R not to employ females on board liners sailing to the Far East. Although the decision was well founded, the Equal Treatment Act still applied. Accordingly it was found that M's rights had been breached and R was ordered to pay compensation, fixed at DKR 10,000.

---

1 Case S 4/1979, U 1980, 328.

In this case, brought on 7 March 1979, the seamen's union in Denmark, hereafter called the union, as representatives of Sonja Jensen claimed that the defendant, the shipping company A.P. Møller, in line with s. 8 of [the Equal Treatment Act], is obliged to pay the plaintiff DKR 12,500, plus normal interest. This amount is compensation for refusing the plaintiff a berth on M/S *Cornelia Mærsk*, belonging to the defendant, on 16 November 1978.

The defendant has made a plea for dismissal of the case on the ground that the case does not come under the Equal Treatment Act.

The particulars in the case are as follows:

The plaintiff, who is 25 years old and living in Haderslev, applied through the job centre in Esbjerg for a berth as an experienced seaman. According to her wish she was assigned a berth on M/S *Mercandian Sun* on 15 November 1978, but was refused by the shipping company on the grounds of the vessel's bath and toilet conditions. On 16 November she was assigned a berth on M/S *Cornelia Mærsk*, but was also refused.

The defendant has in a letter dated 23 February 1979 given the following reasons for the refusal:

> ... The reason why seaman Sonja Jensen could not be employed on board M/S *Cornelia Mærsk* was *inter alia* because in our opinion she could not do the work as a seaman under the conditions prevailing in the tour areas of this vessel.

The timetable shows that, on 19 November 1978, the vessel arrived in Hamburg. From the North European ports it would sail via Suez to Singapore, Labuan, Manila, Hong Kong, Kaohsiung, Keelung, Udsan, Busan, Uno, Kobe, Yokohama, Hong Kong and return via Suez.

The union made an application to the Labour Ministry concerning the two refusals, which were argued to be in breach of the Equal Treatment Act. In the reply from the Ministry, of 29 January 1979, it is stated *inter alia*:

> ... Conditions in foreign places may be seen as a ground for exemption, but a concrete case for exemption must be made in individual cases... .

The union has brought a similar case against Mercandia shipping company. That case will be heard immediately after the present case. In both cases the Equal Status Council intervened in support of the plaintiff's claim. The Ministry of Trade and the Labour Ministry have been informed ... .

During the hearing evidence was given by the plaintiff, by captains in the respondent shipping company, John Guldbrandsen and Bent Eigil Hansen, and by stewardess Tove Valborg Hansen.

The plaintiff explained that she started sailing in 1973. After sea-training school and three years at sea, she got her first berth as efficient deck hand on board ØK's *Arosia* to the Far East in May 1978. She has always worked on an equal footing with her male colleagues, both on the deck and in the hold, day or night, without any real problems. She has sailed to Pakistan, Sri Lanka, the South American rivers and West Africa to the Equator. After having been paid off the *Arosia* in September she immediately looked for a new berth. The first one offered was on the *Mercandian Sun* on 15 November 1978. After the refusal on 16 November 1978 she was not offered another berth until 16 December 1978. She was then hired as holiday relief on board DFDS's *England*.

John M. Guldbrandsen has explained that he was employed by the defendant in 1958 and sailed until 1971 as a navigator mainly to the Far East. It was while he was head of the personnel department in the shipping company that the plaintiff was refused. The shipping company had previously employed female deck hands, and the department was aware of the Equal Treatment Act, which had in principle been accepted. On tankers belonging to the company female deck hands were employed. However, on the company's liners, among them *Cornelia Mærsk*, sailing to the Far East it is considered unsafe, as the nature of the work holds a certain risk for women. This includes especially the night watch when the desk hand is often alone, and the supervision in the hold of local dockworkers. The company has had a trainee female navigator on one of its vessels, but the duties of trainees are not the same as those of deck hands, and can be arranged in such a way that there is little risk.

Bent Nielsen has explained that he has been employed by the defendant for approximately 20 years. He is now chief of the company's technical department. He has for many years sailed to the Far East as navigator and captain, and is of the opinion that problems of safety are involved in having women deck hands on board vessels to the Far East, because of the (according to Western opinion) deviant attitude of the local dockers. There have been problems with a female trainee, who in the Far East was sent into the hold to inspect the work of the dockers, but had to abandon it when she was pawed by the dockers.

The lawyer for the union has, in support of the claim, stated that it is not disputed that the plaintiff was qualified for the employment, and that refusing her did not take place after a genuine evaluation of her qualifications, but because she is a woman. According to s. 1 of the Act, every direct or indirect discrimination between men and women is illegal, and it is therefore ruled out that importance is placed on sex as such or on sex characteristics such as pregnancy, stronger muscles in men etc. The plaintiff does not dispute that there is a greater risk for women than for men working in ports in the Far East, but it must be left to the individual to decide whether to take that risk. The law has abandoned 'gentleman' concepts, which the defendant is expressing. If the defendant really thought that an unacceptably high risk was attached to this employment, a dispensation according to s. 11 should have been sought.

The law does not have scales for compensation according to s. 8. In this case it must be realistic to demand compensation equivalent to that set in s. 18 of the Seamen's Act for unfair dismissal, namely two months' salary.

The Advocate of the Chamber has, on behalf of the Equal Status Council in support of the claim by the plaintiff, stated that the Act clearly includes seamen ... . The law implies that a general refusal to employ women is illegal even in cases where the jobs are dangerous. The reference by the defendant to the shipping route is immaterial, as the refusal is not based on a concrete evaluation of plaintiff's abilities, but exclusively on her sex. No dispensation was sought.

Counsel for the defence has, in support of the plea for dismissal of the case, stated that the defendant after careful consideration has taken the decision not to employ female seamen on his liners sailing to the Far East. It must, according to the evidence given, be regarded certain that a real risk exists for women in that area. It cannot therefore be asserted in this case that no concrete evaluation of plaintiff's qualifications was made.

It appears from the preambles of the Act that work which by its nature must be done by members of a particular sex, such as sex-determined acting roles, fashion modelling or bathing personnel, falls outside the Act without it being necessary to seek dispensation. The examples show that it falls outside the Act if factual reasons for different treatment of the sexes exist. It is a factual reason to have regard to special safety problems on board these liners. Although the refusal to employ the plaintiff was not founded on a concrete evaluation of her suitability for the employment in question, it is not in breach of the Act, as this situation falls outside the application of the Act. There was therefore no reason for the defendant to seek dispensation.

...

The Court decides:

It is not disputed that the refusal of the plaintiff happened as a result of the defendant not wanting to employ female deck hands on board his liners calling at ports in the Far East. Regardless of whether this decision was actually taken for risk reasons regarding the safety of women working on board, it does not imply that the Equal Treatment Act is not applicable. Estimating possible risks related to sex in workplaces outside Denmark is exactly one of the problems for the dispensation authority to deal with, and not for the court.

As the defendant did not seek dispensation, it is found that the plaintiff's rights according to the Act have been violated and the defendant is found to be obliged to pay the plaintiff compensation, in view of the circumstances set at DKR 10,000.

The defendant must pay the costs of DKR 5,000.

8.2.2 SUPREME COURT, HD, 30 MAY 1980

Sømændenes Forbund i Danmark for Sonja J. Jensen mod Mercandia Rederierne[1]

On 24 January 1953 a vessel was given a notice about common rooms etc. for crew members, which ordered installation of separate washrooms with bath for women, but only if there were female personnel on board. This had not previously been the case, and such installations were not made. In spite of this the shipping company was found not to be justified in refusing employment to a female deck hand under the Equal Treatment Act, while it was not found necessary to award the female deck hand compensation, claimed under the Act.

...

Four judges pronounce:

As, it is pointed out, the vessel was furbished according to the provisions in the notice of 1953, and as the Minister did not find occasion under the Equal Treatment Act to amend the set demands, the defendant must have been entitled to refuse female deck hands on the vessels furbished in this manner, otherwise the company would have risked penalties according to s. 42 of the Act of 1951, concerning inspection of ships.

As the defendant employs female deck hands on the newer vessels, no actual intention of discrimination directly or indirectly existed.

For this reason the judges voted for dismissal of the case against the defendant.

Each party to pay its own costs in the case.

---

1 Case II 335/1979, U 1980, 569.

Verdict of the Supreme Court:

The verdict against which this appeal has been taken was issued by the Admiralty and Commercial Court.

Seven judges took part in the judgment: Schaumburg, Urne, Torben Jensen, Bangert, Funch Jensen, Weber and Gersing.

The appellant has maintained to the Supreme Court the claim for the defendant to pay an amount fixed by the Supreme Court in compensation, not exceeding DKR 12,500 plus normal interest. Alternatively, the appellant has made a claim for the defendant to acknowledge that in November 1978 the refusal to employ Sonja Jensen as deck hand on the M/S *Mercandian Sun* was unjustified.

The defendant has claimed ratification of the alternative claim as well.

In the Supreme Court the Equal Status Council intervened in support of the plaintiff's claim.

The Supreme Court was informed that the Labour Minister, in connection with replies to questions put by the Parliamentary Committee about proposals for amendments of various provisions concerning equal treatment of men and women in employment, has declared:

> Question 6:
>
> In how many cases will the re-furbishing of factory buildings, workplaces and planning of facilities for both sexes entail considerable increases in production costs to the company? How does the Minister contemplate the enforcement of the Act and the proposed practice of dispensation?
>
> Answer:
>
> The Labour Ministry does not possess information about the extent to which re-furbishing of factory buildings, workplaces and planning of facilities for both sexes will entail considerable increases in production costs for the companies. As appears from the comments attached to this draft amendment as well as proposals for the Equal Treatment Act, these amendments are necessary for the enforcement of the EEC Directive dated 9 February 1976 which Denmark is obliged to implement before 9 August 1978. It cannot, however, be completely ruled out that some changes in production in connection with the implementation of the Act are so necessary and so extensive that they cannot reasonably be expected to be completed before the Act comes into force.
>
> These very special cases may, according to section 11(1) of the Equal Treatment Act, after concrete evaluation, be given dispensation of a limited period to bring the conditions into compliance with the regulations.

Four judges, Urne, Funch Jensen, Weber and Gersing, declare:

There are no provisions in the Equal Treatment Act exempting the shipping industry from the rules of law, and it was therefore the duty of the defendant, not having a dispensation under s. 11 of the Act, to observe the provision for equal treatment as laid down in s. 2 on employment of ships' crews. It must here be noted that, in the light of the Act and its general aims, it was apparently only intended to tolerate such limitations as are clearly indicated.

The duty to observe equal treatment cannot be regarded as limited by s. 3. The further claim by the appellant regarding notice No 9 of 24 January 1953, paragraph 20(4), concerning separate washrooms for women, is not found to be a sufficient reason to limit the above-mentioned duty. This provision sets a pattern for wash and bathroom conditions 'for female personnel on board' and should by its factual content be applied whether the women are employed with or without obligation to do so. The question was treated in more general terms during the parliamentary debate of the Equal Treatment Act and the proposed amendments, especially in the above-mentioned (but unpublished in the official report of parliamentary proceedings) ministerial statement to the parliamentary committee. It must therefore be presumed that the legislature expected that companies to whom the question might become important had to adapt the workplaces to comply with the equal treatment principle.

The Equal Treatment Act has in a way made it necessary for the affected shipping companies either to obtain dispensation from the Act or to make the necessary arrangements regarding wash and bathroom facilities if they were not to be put in the same situation as has arisen for the defendant, just as it has arisen in many other industries according to the evidence to the Supreme Court by the intervener. There has, therefore, been every reason to suppose that the legal position, which in no way is or was doubtful, had been made clear to the affected parties concerning the introduction of the Act. That this has been neglected can in no way alter the actual legal position.

As a result of this the defendant has, by refusing Sonja Jensen employment, violated the Equal Treatment Act, but for the reasons given in the dissent to the Admiralty and Commercial Court verdict, it must be accepted that no compensation was awarded under s. 8 of the Act. However, it is found that the alternative claim by the appellant, which received no special comment from the defendant, should be complied with.

These judges also dismiss costs for both parties.

Three judges, Schaumburg, Torben Jensen and Bangert, declare:

As stated in the verdict, the vessel, in line with notice No 67 of 28 February 1977, paragraph 2(2), which was unchanged by the introduction of the Equal Treatment Act, still comes under the provisions of notice No 9 of 24 January 1953, according to which it does not fall to the defendant to install separate washrooms with baths for female personnel or to make other suitable arrangements, as no such personnel was on board. It must therefore be assumed that installation of bathroom facilities for female personnel could not be made without structural alterations. It is therefore endorsed that the reasons given in the verdict entitled the defendant to refuse to employ the female deck hand. These judges accordingly vote to endorse the verdict.

Judgment will be made according to the majority vote.

The verdict:

Defendant, the Mercandia Shipping Company, must acknowledge that the refusal to employ deck hand, Sonja F. Jensen, on board M/S *Mercandian Sun* on 15 November 1978 was unfair.

Each party has to pay its own costs in the cases in the Admiralty and Commercial Court and in the Supreme Court.

8.2.3 SUPREME COURT, HD, 15 MARCH 1983

Kvindeligt Arbejderforbund i Danmark
mod Industrifagene og Danpo[1]

In previous agreements between the poultry industry (slaughter) and the Women Workers' Union (KAD), whose members were the sole workers doing conveyor belt work with poultry, it was stated that the supply situation at any time could lead to the employees being sent home without any financial obligation on the employer. In later regulations in connection with common agreements between, on the one side, the employers, and on the other side KAD and the Special Workers' Union (SiD), a similar regulation existed, but it was limited to the area which, until 1 January 1976, was covered by the KAD agreement. This regulation was not found to be in breach of Act No 161 of 12 April 1978 which was introduced under an EEC Directive, as the 'sending home option' was factually based on the supply of raw materials, and the regulation had to be seen as covering employees of both sexes within the area previously covered by KAD, regardless of the union of which they were members (Dissent).

Eastern Division of the High Court: Verdict, 28 January 1981
(Graulund Hansen, Kjær, Bodil Wiingaard).

Following the agreements which had for a number of years been negotiated between first defendant, the trade industries, as employers and the plaintiff, *Kvindeligt Arbejderforbund i Danmark* (KAD) and the Danish General Workers' Union (SiD) as workers' organizations, in such a way that agreements were reached separately with the two unions, a common

---

1 Case II 58/1981, U 1983, 379.

agreement between the first defendant and both unions was negotiated. This agreement was renewed in 1979. In the agreement in force until 1976 between the first defendant and the plaintiff concerning notice of dismissal (agreed in 1971) para. 6 states:

> As the workers' side has acknowledged that the area of agreement at present covers seasonal work, in which the supply situation may at any time lead to the need to send the workers home without financial responsibility on the employer, it is also acknowledged that final termination of employment is subject to the following notices:
> - from the workers' side:
>   - seven days after one year's employment
>   - 14 days after two years' employment
> - from the employers' side:
>   - seven days after one year's employment and more.

This formula, which had no parallel in the old SiD agreement, was not repeated in the common agreement of 1977. On the basis of paragraph 52 (1979 agreement paragraph 54) the parties passed a number of special resolutions, in which point H states:

> Within the area which was until 1 January 1976 covered by the KAD agreement, the supply situation may at any time cause the employees to be sent home without financial obligation on the employer.

The employers' organization, the Trade Industries, includes amongst its members the defendant, Danpo A/S, which at present runs four establishments, Ringsted Fjerfabrik (Feather Works), Vamdrup Fjerkræslagteri (slaughterhouse), Vamdrup Fjerfabrik and Hasle Fjerkræslagteri, while the slaughterhouse in Ars has an agreement in accordance with the special provision in point H.

The historical background to the 'sending home' provision is that the parties in 1959 agreed for the first time on conditions for giving notice to terminate employment, and that this provision had not fully suited the poultry industry's special circumstances, as supply of poultry was fluctuating and totally dependent on deliveries from individual farmers. On the basis of the provision the slaughter houses may, where conveyor belts systems are used, send home without pay members of the KAD when the supply fails, but not members of SiD.

In 1974 the EEC Council of Ministers decided, in connection with its Directive on working and social conditions, to take steps to secure the implementation of equality between men and women regarding access to employment, vocational training, promotion and working conditions, including remuneration. Regarding the latter, the Council passed a Directive on 10 February 1975 implementing throughout the Member States the principle of equal pay for men and women.

The Directive was implemented in Denmark by Act No 32 of 4 February 1976. Furthermore, a Council Directive of 9 February 1976 concerning the implementation of the principle of equal treatment between men and women regarding access to employment, vocational training, promotion and working conditions was passed. This Directive forms the basis of Act No 161, dated 12 April 1978 on equal treatment between men and women regarding employment etc. In s. 1 it provides: 'For the purpose of this Act equal treatment of men and women means that no discrimination may take place on the grounds of sex.' Section 4 of the Act provides: 'An employer who employs men and women shall treat them equally as regards working conditions. This shall also apply in connection with dismissal.' According to s. 11, provisions in agreements and in the firms' regulations which are in breach of ss. 2 to 5, are illegal.

During the collective negotiations in the spring of 1979 the plaintiff tried without success to get the defendant to omit the special provision. When this was not successful, the plaintiff reserved this right to let the compatibility of the provision with the Equal Treatment Act be tested by the courts. In this case, brought by summons for hearing on 18 December 1979, the plaintiff has sought that the defendant be obliged to acknowledge that the 'sending home' provision under point H in the agreement of 1977 and in the renewal of 1979 violates Act No 161 of 12 April 1978 and is therefore illegal.

The defendant has pleaded for dismissal of the case.

Evidence has been given by Mrs Agnes Gejl of Vamdrup, Mrs Tove Andersen of Ullits, Mrs Edith Andersen of Hasle, department leader Agnes Nielsen of Ringsted and area manager Jens Tage Sørensen of Vamdrup.

Mrs Agnes Gejl has explained that she has been employed at Vamdrup Fjerkræslagteri for 21 years as a packer. The poultry is brought in in the morning and hung up by the women workers. The entire process is done on a conveyor belt by the women. There are, however, a few men driving the processed poultry to the cold store, and one man helps in the cutting up area. The witness believes that 30 to 40 women work at the conveyor belt. On days when there are no more poultry left the women are sent home, which happens often. If they are without work for a certain number of hours in a week, they receive unemployment benefit. The supplies are never sufficient for a whole week's work. The men stay when the women are sent home and presumably do the cleaning up etc.

Mrs Tove Andersen explained that she has been employed for just over two years in the packing department at Danpo in Års. Here men unload the poultry from the vehicles and hang up the live chickens, just as it is the men who knife the chickens which did not die in the slaughter machine. After veterinary inspection the rest of the work on the conveyor belt is carried out by women. Thirty-two women are employed in the slaughter house with 23 to 24 men. In the cutting-up department 60 to 70 women and a few men work. The witness believes that about 120 women and 32 men work in the slaughter house. The men are all members of SiD, while the women are members of the prosecuting union. When the slaughter has ended for the day, the women are sent home without pay, while the men stay. If the women are sent home for more than eight hours during one week, they receive 90 per cent of their wages in unemployment benefit.

Mrs Edith Rasmussen explained that she has been employed at Danpo in Hasle for 15 years, and has worked in the cutting-up department with five other women. In this slaughterhouse two male workers do the unloading and the hanging, and one male worker transports the ready packed chickens to the cold store. The women are always sent home when slaughtering is finished. Sometimes the male workers are sent home too. This may happen about 25 times a year, while there are no limits to the number of lay-offs for women.

Department leader Agnes Nielsen explained that she has not worked herself at Danpo's factory in Ringsted, where the poultry slaughter will close down on 1 January 1980. Both men and women worked there. All the men were members of SiD and all the women were members of KAD. In 1979 the women when laid off received unemployment benefit, if they were sent home for at least four hours per week. The number of hours has now been doubled. In borderline cases Danpo arranged the working so that the women could get benefits.

Area manager Jens Tage Sørensen explained that he is employed as production manager in Danpo and at the same time as leader of Vamdrup Fjerkræslagteri, where some 130 women are employed. When the slaughtering has ended the women clock off and go home. The canteen ladies and women not working at the conveyor belt are not sent home. There are no reasons for the firm not to employ women members of SiD, but a female member of SiD was ordered by the plaintiff and the other female employees to transfer to KAD. The witness does not know the background to this, but believes that it may be due to an agreement between the two unions. The slaughterhouse has, according to agreement with SiD, the right to lay off male workers for a total of 35 days per year, the so-called work sharing. This work sharing agreement has, however, to be re-negotiated every year.

The plaintiff, in support of the claim, has stressed that it is in breach of s. 4 of the Equal Treatment Act that women workers, according to point H of the agreement, risk being laid off without pay, when the male workers in the same work place do not run that risk. According to comments on the Bill, the invalidity rules in s. 7 also include collective agreements, such as the one disputed in this case. As it appears from information received in this case, the men and women employed at Danpo do the same work during the slaughtering, and the male workers do the incidental work of clearing up or gardening, while the women are sent home. The plaintiff does not dispute that factual reasons for unequal treatment may exist in the same place of work, for example where such different kinds of work are carried out as heavy blacksmith and canteen work, but these differences cannot be used in support of unequal treatment. It is of no importance how many workers of each sex are working at the conveyor belt in poultry slaughter department, as it is conclusive that the lay-off provision affects women. In the judgment of this case it is also of no importance that the women have the option of unemployment benefits, and that some of them may be interested in this arrangement. Neither should it influence the judgment, that the women, according to an agreement between the unions, are all enrolled in the plaintiff union rather than the SiD. It is not important either that the male workers can have 35 days free of slaughtering a year, as these days are pre-arranged as holidays, and therefore do not remove the inequality. The special provision clearly entails a different arrangement for women from that of men working in the same place, and this happens in spite of the two sexes carrying out the same work. According to the present limited legal practice, strong factual reasons are required to deviate from the Equal Treatment Act. In the present case, the only factual ground is that special treatment for women cuts production costs, in that there is a saving on the wages bill when the workers are sent home before the end of normal working hours. It is stressed that it is exactly such circumstances that the Act seeks to counter-act. The plaintiff does not claim compensation or punishment, although the Equal Treatment Act warrants that. The plaintiff only wants a fundamental agreement on whether the regulations for lay-off breach the Act, and if so that they be declared unlawful. It is denied that the plaintiff, by only enrolling women members, has itself breached the act, which does not aim at these conditions.

The defendant has, in support of the plea for dismissal of the case, stressed that the collective agreement with its special provisions was entered into between organizations with equal rights on the labour market. The condition included in the Equal Treatment Act is therefore not respected when an employer differentiates between individual workers in his employment. Lay-off regulations have long traditions within the poultry industry as well as in many other areas, such as filleting of fish and roofing felt manufacture, where male workers often face lay-offs without pay. There is nothing to prevent the parties from negotiating an agreement, except that the plaintiff may have to relinquish some of the benefits which the present agreement gives its members. The dispute arose in the first place because the plaintiff union — presumably in contravention of the Equal Treatment Act — only enrols women members, and the problem would not exist if the women employed in the poultry industry were members of SiD. This could be arranged without problems, as the above-mentioned union, which covers the same areas as the plaintiff, does not make gender a condition for membership. According to point H of the agreement, the supply situation determines the lay-offs. The difference in treatment does not happen because the workers are women, but because of the nature of the work and of fluctuations in delivery. The Equal Treatment Act will only touch on the differential treatment in terms of sex discrimination, and in this case it has not been breached. When the male workers at the conveyor belt in the slaughterhouse are not laid off at the end of slaughtering, it is not due to their sex but merely because their union SiD has an agreement containing other provisions than that of the plaintiff, possibly because the disputed work is mainly done by women, and that laying off men was of no great importance to the firms. It is therefore not a case of over-manning and laying off of surplus workers. In cases like that the terms of the collective agreement must be adhered to on dismissal. That the lay-offs hit all those who are doing the same kind of work clearly shows that the conditions are factually founded. The male workers do not take over the work of the laid-off women, as there simply is no work to take over and as the work could not be done by inexperienced men. The dissatisfaction among the plaintiff's members may, in the defendants' opinion, lie in the fact that the right to unemployment benefit has been changed, so that a worker must have been laid off for at least eight hours to get benefit, while four hours had previously been enough. The Courts must be wary of forcing changes in collective agreements. The trade unions have enough power to take care of their own interests when negotiating renewal of agreements, and it is in this area that the present problem lies. The defendant considers it unreasonable and in breach of the Equal Treatment Act that the union enrols only women members ... . The defendant admits that the regulations for lay-offs have financial connotations, but are not based on criteria of sex. It is stressed that the Equal Treatment Act does not aim at the collective agreements, although it is not disputed that provisions in these fields may be included in the Act.

The High Court will pronounce:

Regulations in collective agreements must, if they are in breach of the rules set down in the Equal Treatment Act, be regarded as unlawful to the same extent as individual agreements between employers and employees.

The evidence shows that Danpo A/S employs workers of both sexes for the same work, and that the male workers, who are all members of SiD, are not laid off if the slaughtering is completed before the end of the normal working hours. The evidence has also shown that SiD enrols members of both sexes, while the plaintiff according to its rules only enrols women members.

If point H of the agreement had been formulated in such a way that Danpo, due to the supply situation, had a right to send the women workers home without pay, but not the men doing the same kind of work, that provision would have been in breach of s. 4 of the Equal Treatment Act, and as a result the plaintiff's claim would have been upheld under s. 7 of the Act.

However, the agreement in point H, which according to information has been copied from the previous agreement between *Industrifagene* and *Kvindeligt Arbejderforbund* to this collective agreement, is formulated in such a way that it only applies to the members of this union and not to previous members of SiD. The fact that workers are sent home is therefore due to their membership of the plaintiff union, and it is irrelevant to the defendant that this union only enrols female workers.

Following the evidence given by Jens Tage Sørensen, it is not required by the defendants that the women be members of the plaintiff's union, as this depends on an agreement between the two workers' organizations. The different treatment between men and women, which takes place in the defendants' firms, is caused by union conditions, and not by the employers' sex discrimination. As the differential treatment is a consequence of union rules, the plaintiff union is found to have no legal reason to claim that the Equal Treatment Act has been breached.

We therefore find that the case against the defendant should be dismissed.

...

Verdict by the Supreme Court:

The appealed verdict is given by *Østre Landsret* (Supreme Court, Eastern Division).

The decision was reached by seven judges: Høyrup, Urne, Bjerregaard, Torben Jensen, Munch, Kardel and Else Mols.

The appellant has repeated the claim. The defendant has asked for the dismissal of the case.

In the Supreme Court the Equal Status Council intervened in support of plaintiff's claim.

The defendants have as their main point stated that point H in the special provision, by its wording, allows the option to lay off workers employed within the special area, which until 1 January 1976 was covered by the KAD agreement. The lay-off option is factually founded on the supply conditions of the raw materials, and does not constitute any discrimination of workers on sex grounds. Male workers employed within this area may also be laid off. The defendants have declared that women workers not employed in this area cannot be sent home.

New evidence has been brought to the Supreme Court.

The collective agreement does not contain provisions which give the appellant special benefits over members of SiD.

Five judges, Høyrup, Urne, Bjerregaard, Torben Jensen and Else Mols, pronounce:

According to the claim by the appellant this case concerns the question whether the special provision point H is in breach of the Equal Treatment Act.

According to its wording, point H deals with the area which until 1976 was covered by the KAD agreement, and the provision, as part of the collective agreement, is seen to include both sexes working within the same area, regardless of the sex of the member concerned. The option to lay off members within this area is dependent on supply of raw materials. The provision is therefore not found to be in breach of the Equal Treatment Act, and the judges vote to affirm the judgment. They also vote for each party to pay its own costs in the case.

The judges Munch and Kardel pronounce:

The special provision covers the work which, until 1976, traditionally was women's work, and the defendants have acknowledged that this work remains entirely women's work, with a few exceptions. The option of lay-offs does not however affect work which traditionally is done by men, even in the cases where this work also depends on supplies. These judges therefore do not find that the defendants have proven that the difference in treatment depends on factual considerations. The provision under these circumstances entails such a different treatment of women that it must be seen as being in breach of the Equal Treatment Act. Therefore, they vote to uphold the claim by the plaintiff.

Judgment will be passed according to majority vote.

The verdict:

The verdict of the High Court will stand.

Each party will meet its own costs.

8.2.4 HIGH COURT, ØLD, 7 DECEMBER 1981

John Bøgh mod Specialarbejderforbundet i Danmark[1]

As a result of the agreement which the Ministry of Finance had entered into with SiD and KAD respectively, and which was valid for reception centre F, only women and not men under 55 could get part-time employment. A, who was for this reason refused part-time employment by F, claimed that SiD and the Ministry of Finance should be obliged to acknowledge that the relevant provision in the SiD agreement was unlawful. Although it was no longer of interest to A to seek the above-mentioned employment, and regardless of the fact that the term in the agreement had lapsed since the case was brought to court, it was accepted that A had sufficient interest in this problem for it to be brought before the court.[2]

Male employees were refused part-time employment at the rehabilitation centre F under a provision in the collective agreement entered into between the Ministry of Finance and SiD. According to this agreement, only workers over 55 years of age could be employed. A similar limitation to part-time employment did not apply to the women employed by F, as the agreement between the Ministry and KAD did not contain such a provision. In the case which A brought against SiD and the Ministry of Finance, claiming that the provision in the agreement was unlawful, it was argued to be a breach of the Equal Treatment Act that men and women did not have the same right to part-time employment; but as the term in the above-mentioned agreement, considered in isolation, was not found to be breach of the Act, the case against the defendants was dismissed.

The plaintiff, John Bøgh, born on 11 January 1953, had during the summer of 1978, while he was a polytechnic student, been employed as a temporary worker at the reception centre Ebberødgård (now Svaneparken). When a position became vacant on 1 February 1979 as part-time night-watch for 16 hours per week, the plaintiff applied for this job but was refused on the ground that male employees at the centre were employed under the rules set out in the agreement between the defendant, *Specialarbejderforbundet* (SiD) and the Ministry of Finance, and these rules did not permit part-time employment of men under 55 years of age.

The plaintiff protested to SiD, as he maintained that enforcement of this provision in his situation would be a breach of s. 2 [of the Equal Treatment Act], as no restrictions on part-time employment existed in the agreement between *Kvindeligt Arbejderforbund i Danmark* and the Ministry of Finance, according to which employment of women took place at the centre.

1 Case 9-633/1979, U 1982, 484.

2 See GOMARD: *Civilprocessen*, pp. 170-171 and 193-195.

SiD's reply was that employment in the above-mentioned position would be a breach of the agreement, and when the plaintiff applied for membership of KAD, he was given the reply that he should contact SiD with his problem.

The plaintiff put the case to the Ministry of Labour, informing them that the inspector at Ebberødgård had told him that he would have got the job if the agreements with the unions had not prevented it.

The reply from the Ministry of Labour dated 27 June 1979 states:

> The Ministry of Labour has in order to reply to your letter obtained statements from *Specialarbejderforbundet* (SiD), *Kvindeligt Arbejderforbund* (KAD), the Ministry of Social Affairs and the Finance Ministry's Department for Remuneration and Pensions.
>
> SiD stated that KAD and SiD have entered into separate agreements with the remuneration and pension department of the Ministry of Finance on the basis of what is in the best interests of the unions' members. SiD is aware of the existing KAD agreement on part-time employment, and that it is not included in SiD's agreement.
>
> SiD also stated that when you [the plaintiff] cannot be accepted for part-time employment, the reason is that no agreement on pay and conditions for part-time work exists in SiD's agreement with the Finance Ministry.
>
> KAD has stated that the union does not consider itself to be in breach of the Equal Treatment Act regarding the part-time employment, as the union does not prevent men from working within the agreement areas. It is the opinion of the union that in the present circumstances you [the plaintiff] must seek membership of another union.
>
> The Ministry of Social Affairs has, in an exchange of letters with the Social Administration, stated that the employment of unskilled night-watch persons takes place according to agreements with SiD and KAD, in as much as men are employed under the SiD agreement, while women are employed under the KAD agreement.
>
> The Ministry of Social Affairs has furthermore stated that the two agreements contain different provisions for working hours, as the KAD agreement provides for part-time employment, while there is no provision for part-time work for persons under the age of 55 in the SiD agreement. As it involves part-time work, the job for which you [the plaintiff] applied can, in the opinion of the Ministry of Social Affairs, only go to a person remunerated in accordance with the KAD agreement. The Remuneration and Pensions Department of the Finance Ministry has stated that the Ministry has negotiated with the *Specialarbejderforbundet* (SiD) and the institutions involved in order to ensure that its agreement with the union in question does not constitute a breach of the Equal Treatment Act.
>
> Following these negotiations, the Finance Ministry stated that it was not possible to enter into agreement with the union regarding your [the plaintiff's] possible part-time employment on night duty at the reception centre for North Zealand.
>
> In this connection it must be mentioned that in the opinion of the Labour Ministry it is in breach of the Equal Treatment Act that the agreement conditions at

> the reception centre have prevented you [the plaintiff] from obtaining employment on part-time night duty on equal footing with women.

In this connection the Labour Ministry refers to s. 7 of the Equal Treatment Act, according to which provisions in agreements contravening the regulations in the Act are unlawful. Naturally this also applies to collective agreements. In a reply to the Labour Market Committee the Labour Minister declared that in areas covered by agreements for men and women respectively, which when compared with each other show discrimination in breach of the Equal Treatment Act, a case for nullity of these provisions can be brought before the courts; this also include questions of general contraventions of the Equal Treatment Act.

An enquiry from the plaintiff to the Social Administration, whether he could expect to be considered for the next vacant part-time job, was replied to by the Social Administration's letter of 12 July 1979; it stated that the Administration had to follow the agreements entered into by the Finance Ministry, agreements which the plaintiff could possibly seek to have overruled by the courts.

In a letter to the advocate for the plaintiff, dated 9 November 1979, the Finance Ministry stated that it had nothing against male workers under the age of 55 being employed part-time, but that it had not been possible to persuade SiD about this matter.

The advocate for the plaintiff contacted the Equal Status Council, who by letter of 28 November 1979, replied:

> The Equal Status Council finds it to be in breach of section 2 of the Equal Treatment Act where the terms of agreements at the reception centre for North Zealand lead to men not being employed on part-time, unskilled night duty work, while women are.

Seen in isolation, the SiD and the KAD agreements cannot be considered in breach of the Equal Treatment Act in the context of allowing or not allowing part-time work. The fact that KAD does not take male members, and the application of the SiD and KAD agreements respectively to real work conditions and places, are the causes of discrimination in the employment situation.

In this case, brought on 28 December 1979, the plaintiff, who has been granted legal aid, claims that the defendants, SiD and the Finance Ministry, must be obliged to acknowledge 'that the agreement entered into by the defendants before 28 October 1981 is unlawful as regards the provision that men under the age of 55 cannot be employed part-time'.

The plaintiff has reserved the right to claim compensation.

The defendants have made a plea for rejection or, alternatively, dismissal of the case.

The agreement in question between the Finance Ministry and SiD was entered into on 12 December 1977 and covers, amongst other things, employment under the Social Administration. Paragraph 1 of the agreement states:

> Normal work is 40 hours per week. ...
>
> Part-time employment with proportional remuneration can take place for workers over the age of 55, on the basis of previous negotiations between the institution and the union.

The agreement was replaced by another agreement dated 28 November 1979, in which the same terms were repeated.

The agreement between the Finance Ministry and KAD was entered into on 22 July 1977 and includes in paragraph 1 a provision about working hours being up to 40 per week.

After the care of handicapped persons was transferred to the districts, a new agreement was entered into by the Association of County Councils in Denmark with both SiD and KAD and other unions with effect from 1 January 1980. This agreement corresponded in the main to the previous agreements, but it has now been succeeded by another agreement dated 28 October 1981, under which SiD members have the option of part-time employment, as in regard to work hours it only states that the average weekly hours are 40.

During the proceedings the plaintiff has explained that after having had his application refused, he continued on supply duty for about two months. His pay for this was approximately DKR 2,000 less than he could have earned in the job for which he applied. After the two months he got a 'tailor-made' job as week-end watchman with roughly the same pay as he could have had in the job he was refused, but with less suitable hours. He was later, possibly from January 1980, employed full-time. He finished at the end of 1980 when he passed his examination.

In support of his claim the plaintiff has stated that the term in the agreement has prevented him from being employed part-time, while there was no hindrance to women being employed in the job. This is — as stated by the Labour Ministry and the Equal Status Council — in clear breach of s. 2 in the Equal Treatment Act, and the agreement provision must therefore be regarded as unlawful according to the same Act.

The defendants have, in support of their plea, stated that the plaintiff having completed his studies is no longer interested in employment at the centre, and also that the agreement provision in question is no longer valid. The plaintiff has therefore lost his interest in the question.

The defendant SiD has, regarding the plea for dismissal of the case, denied that the term in the agreement is in breach of the Equal Treatment Act. Part-time work is generally regarded by the unions as undesirable, and the fact that KAD's agreement on this point was inferior to the valid SiD agreement cannot be a reason to disregard the latter. Apart from this, an overall view must be taken when judging various agreements within the same area — as it was remarked in the preambles of the Act — in order that benefits to one sex in certain areas can be compensated for by benefits to the other sex in different areas.

The Finance Ministry has, for its part, as further support of the plea for rejection, stated that the Ministry has, since the introduction of community care for the handicapped, not been a party to negotiations and is therefore not the real defendant. In support of the plea for dismissal the Ministry has stated that the SiD agreement in itself does not breach the Act, but that the plaintiff's problem only arose from the two agreements, which applied to men and women respectively at that particular place of work, having different provisions for part-time employment. The plaintiff's claim can therefore not be accepted in the way it is formulated.

The Court finds that the plaintiff has the necessary legal interest in having the question legally resolved, and that the question should also justifiably be addressed to the Finance Ministry. The plea for rejection cannot therefore be upheld.

It is agreed that it is in breach of s. 2 of the Equal Treatment Act that the plaintiff, on the ground of a provision in the agreement together with the fact that employment of men at the reception centre could only take place under the rules of the SiD agreement, was cut off from part-time employment, while according to the KAD agreement nothing prevented women from taking up this kind of employment.

As the agreement provision in question, however, ... when seen in isolation, cannot be regarded as being in breach of the Act, the claim by the plaintiff cannot be upheld.

The costs in the case are cancelled.

8.2.5 RECRUITMENT AND DISMISSAL OF PREGNANT WOMEN

Dismissal on grounds of pregnancy or parental leave is prohibited not only in the Equal Treatment Act but also in the Act on Parental Leave. There are a number of cases on pregnant women, which are presented here in summarized form.

8.2.5.1 U 1981, 729 VLD

Around 1 December 1978 the accountancy firm R made an agreement with clerk F to work full-time in the firm from 1 May to September 1979. This was due to the fact that two employees in the firm were to go on maternity leave. It was also agreed that F was to work half-time from January to 1 May. On 23 March 1979, when F informed R that she was also pregnant, she was dismissed on the grounds that she could not honour the agreement on full-time employment during the absence of the other two employees. It was doubtful whether F was aware of her pregnancy at the time when the agreement was made. Therefore the dismissal which was based on the grounds of the pregnancy was in breach of s. 4 of the Equal Treatment Act. Pursuant to s. 8 of the Act F was awarded compensation of DKR 15,000.

8.2.5.2 U 1982, 291 SHD

F had been employed as a clerk at A's premises since 1 July 1978. On 30 January 1981 she was dismissed with effect from the end of April 1981. As it was obvious to assume that pregnancy was the real reason for the dismissal and not reorganisation of work as A maintained, A was ordered, in pursuance of the Equal Treatment Act, to pay compensation which was fixed at DKR 25,000.

8.2.5.3 U 1983, 1063 SHD

In a reduction of personnel in the firm A, salaried worker F alone was dismissed. It was considered that the decision to dismiss her was influenced by the information that she was pregnant. By dismissing F, A had therefore acted in defiance of the Equal Treatment Act and was obliged to pay F compensation. In the light of the circumstances, such as F's relatively short period of service, the compensation was fixed at DKR 10,000.

8.2.5.4 U 1984, 749 HD

As an office clerk at K's premises, F dealt partly with ordinary office work and partly with packing of goods for dispatch. During her pregnancy F was advised by her doctor to avoid hard physical work as she had previously had spontaneous abortions. F was dismissed because she was not in a position to do her normal job perfectly. There was no basis to assume that F's reduction in her ability to work was a result of illness or other reasons unrelated to pregnancy. Consequently there was a violation of the Equal Treatment Act and F, who had been employed for about three years and whose monthly pay was just under DKR 7,000, was given DKR 15,000 under s. 8 of the Act.

8.2.5.5 U 1986, 425

In this case the local council refused continuation of appointment for a woman social worker in a kind of substitute rotation employment. The reason was that the person in question would be absent for about half the time the substitute post was to last because of maternity leave.

The social worker had been a substitute worker for about two years, was clearly well-qualified and was among the applicants who had the longest seniority in the social aid department in question.

The Equal Status Council asked for an opinion on the matter from the local council. Because the case was of such an important nature the Labour Ministry was also asked to give its opinion. The Ministry stated that s. 2 of the Equal Treatment Act affects all terms of appointment including substitute posts. If the purpose of appointment would be lost by appointing a pregnant woman, then the employer could apply for exemption.

The Gladsaxe civil court discharged the municipality from the compensation claim made by the social workers' trade union. The court did not consider it as a notice of termination as the trade union stated. It also did not find that the municipality had violated s. 2 of the Equal Treatment Act by not appointing the social worker for a substitute post lasting just under 8.5 months, of which she could only count on being in position to do her work in the last three months. The court added that absence on account of maternity leave may in this respect be placed on an equal footing with other absence (such as absence because of participation in a course, military service or sickness) which causes the person in question to be cut off from doing the substitute work for much of the period.

The Danish social workers trade union appealed the judgment to the *Østre Landsret* which, on 27 January 1986 confirmed Gladsaxe civil court's judgment. Among other things the High Court stated that the municipality knew that the applicant was pregnant when the decision was to be taken on the appointment to the substitute post. The High Court added that she was entitled to 18 weeks' maternity leave within the period of the substitute post. The High Court stated:

> Referring to the fact that it was clear beforehand that the applicant would not be able to fulfil the position for a great part of the substitute post period, the respondent (the municipality) was found, under these circumstances, to have been correct in not appointing the social worker.

The High Court agreed that not being appointed did not imply dismissal, but it did not accept the civil court's placing of absence on account of maternity leave on equal footing with participation in a course, military service and sickness.

8.2.5.6 Court of Rødovre, 11 December 1987

A woman was employed as a saleswoman on 29 January 1986, and dismissed on 27 February 1986. The employer's reason for dismissal was that the woman had kept her pregnancy secret during the job interview. She gave birth at the end of May. The employer was ordered to pay compensation of DKR 7,000.

8.2.5.7 U 1988, 385 SH

On 16 February1984, F was employed at A's premises as a receptionist earning a salary of DKR 8,750 a month. On 31 August 1984, A informed F that she could possibly take over a vacant job as sales secretary.

On 27 September 1984, A requested F to resign. A was at that time aware that F was pregnant. On 2 October 1984 F refused to resign and she was dismissed on 17 October 1984, with effect from the end of January 1985. F claimed compensation of DKR 25,000 under the Act on maternity leave. A claimed dismissal of the case and stated that they had made a decision on dismissal on 10 September 1984, or in any case that it was before they were aware that F was pregnant. A was found not to have proved that the dismissal decision was made before she was known to be pregnant. F's statement was accepted because A had not objected to the Supreme Court to the amount of compensation.

9. DOCUMENTATION

9.1 BIBLIOGRAPHY

9.1.1 BOOKS, ARTICLES AND REPORTS

ANDERSEN, AGNETE and NIELSEN, RUTH, *Ligestillingslovene med kommentarer*, 1st edition, Copenhagen, 1986; 2nd edition, Copenhagen, 1990.

BRUUN, NIKLAS and KOSKINEN, PIRKKO, *Jämställdhetslagen*, Helsinki, 1987.

CALLEMAN, CATHARINA, LAGERCRANTZ, LENA, PETERSSON, ANN, and WIDERBERG, KARIN, *Kvinnoreformer på mannens vilkor*, Lund, 1984.

DAHL, TOVE STANG, 'Women's right to money', *Working papers in women's law*, Oslo, 1983.

DAHL, TOVE STANG (ed.), *Kvinnerett I + II*, Oslo, 1985.

DAHL, TOVE STANG, GRAVER, KJERSTI, HELLUM, ANNE, and ROBBERTSTAD, ANNE, *Juss and Juks. En arbeidsbok i likestilling*, Oslo, 1975.

DAHL, TOVE STANG *et al*., *Husmorrett, Kvinnerettslige studier*, Oslo, 1981.

DAHLBERG, ANITA,
— 'Jämställdhet - förtryck eller gynnande?', in *Årbog for Kvinderet*, Copenhagen, 1980.
— 'Lagstiftning om planering av arbetsmarknaden', in *Kvinder og offentlig planlægning*. Rapport fra IV. Nordiske Kvindejuristmøde, Århus, 1981.
— 'The Equality Act', in Women's Law in Scandinavia, EWL, No 1, Copenhagen, 1982.
— 'Jämställdhetslagens tillämpning', in *Årborg for Kvinderet*, Copenhagen, 1983.
— *Jämt och ibland*, Stockholm, 1984.
— *Organisation och Styrning*, Stockholm, 1986.

EDELBERG, EINAR, 'Ligebehandlingsloven', in *Årbog for Kvinderet*, Copenhagen, 1979.

FORBURKER- AND ADMINISTRASJONSDEPARTEMENTET, *Opfølgning af handlingsplan for likestilling*, Oslo, 1982.

FORSELL, HARRIET and ÅGREN, KARIN, *Lag om jämställdhed mellan kvinnor och män i arbetslivet — Tillämpning och kommentar*, Paper, University of Umeá, 1982.

FROST, LIS, and PANTMANN, MERETE, 'Deltidsarbejde — ligebehandling', in *Årbog for Kvinderet*, Copenhagen,1980.

HALVORSEN, MARIT,
— 'Om likestillingslovens' § 4, 2. ledd, in *Årbog for Kvinderet*, Copenhagen, 1981.
— 'Om likestillingslovens' § 4, 2. ledd, *Kvinnerettslige Studier*, No 20, Oslo, 1982.
— 'Diskriminering ved ansettelser', in *Kvinnerett II*, Oslo, 1985.
— 'Kjønn and lønn', in *Kvinnerett II*, Oslo, 1985.
— *Sex and Salary*, Oslo, 1988.

HALVORSEN, MARIT, and NIELSEN, RUTH, *Fagbevægelsen og Ligestillingsretten i Norden*, Copenhagen, 1988.

HOLGERSEN, GUDRUN,
— *Likestillingsloven*, Oslo, 1984.
— 'Den Norske Likestillingsloven', in *Årbog for Kvinderet*, Copenhagen, 1980.

HVIDTFELDT, KIRSTEN *et al.* (eds), *Strategies for integrating women into the labour market*, Copenhagen, 1982.

JOHNUNG, CHRISTIANA, *Policies of 'positive discrimination' in Scandinavia in respect of women's employment*, Meddelande 1978:52, Nationalekonomiska Inst., Lunds Universitet, 1978.

KJELLEVOLD, ALICE, MELGARD, SISSEL, and WINNEM, MARIT, *Kvinners rett til arbeid*, Inst. for privatrett, stencilserie No 43, Oslo, 1976.

KØNSROLLEUDVALGET, Undervisningsministeriet, *En vej til ligestilling — positiv særbehandling*, Copenhagen, 1982.

LIGESTILLINGSRÅDET,
— *Årsberetning* 1975/76, 1977, 1978, 1979, 1980, 1981, 1982, 1983, 1984, 1985, 1986, 1987, 1988, Copenhagen.
— *Equal Status of Women in Denmark*, Copenhagen, 1980.
— *Kønskvotering — fortrinsret — positiv særbehandling — aktive foranstaltninger — et forsøg på begrebsafklaring*, Paper, kontaktkonference 1982, Copenhagen, 1982.

LIKESTILLINGSOMBUDET, *Årsmelding* 1979, 1980, 1981, 1982, 1983, 1984, 1985, Oslo.

LIKESTILLINGSRÅDET,
— *Årsmelding* 1978, 1979, 1980, 1981, 1982, 1983, Oslo.
— *Forslag til handlingplan for likestilling*, Oslo, 1980.
— *Nordisk opfølgning af handlingsprogrammet for likestilling fra FN's Kvinnekonferanse i København 1980*, Rapport fra konferanse for offentlige likestillingsorganer i de nordiske lande i sept. 1981, Oslo, 1982.
— *Likestilling i arbeidslivet*, Rapport fra kontaktkonferanse med organisasjonene, Oslo, 1982.
— *Kjønskvotering — et debathefte*, Oslo, 1983.

LINDGARD, JYTTE *et al.* (ed.), *Årbog for Kvinderet* 1978, 1979, 1980, 1981, 1982, 1983, 1984, 1985, Copenhagen.

LO (Swedish),
— *This is how we work for equality between men and women in working life and in the trade unions*, Stockholm, 1980.
— *Jämställdhed och solidaritet. LO's rapport om jämställdhed i arbetslivet och facket*, Stockholm, 1981.

MINISTRY OF EDUCATION, 'En vej til ligestilling — positiv særbehandling,' *Udvalget vedrørende kønsroller og uddannelse*, No 4, Copenhagen, 1982.

NIELSEN, RUTH,
— *Kvindearbejdsret*, Copenhagen, 1979.
— 'Special protective legislation for women in the Nordic countries', in *International Labour Review*, vol. 119, No 1, Geneva, 1980.
— 'Equality in Working Life: Legislation, Positive Action and Introduction of New Technology', in 'Women's Law in Scandinavia', *European Women's Law*, No 1, 1982, col. 112-114.
— *Ledelsesret og ligestilling*, Copenhagen, 1986.
— *EF-arbejdsret*, Copenhagen, 1992.
— *Den svenska jämställdhetslagstiftningen i europeiskt perspektiv*, Copenhagen, 1989.

NIELSEN, RUTH, and PRECHT, KIRSTEN, *EF-regler om ligeløn — perspektiver for dansk ret*, U 1988, B 169.

NORDBORG, GUDRUN,
— *Jämställdhed*, Paper, Umeá University, 1982.
— *Jämställdhed — synspunkter utifrån jämställdhetslagstiftningen och vissa ärenden hos jämställdhets ombudsmannen*, Svensk Juristtidning, 1983.

PETERSEN, HANNE,
— 'Arbejdsretten, staten og kvinderne. Fagretlig praksis vedrørende kvinder i offentlige overenskomstforhold', in *Årbog for Kvinderet*, 1984.
— *Ligestillingslovgivning og kollektive aftaler*, Studier No 5, Retsvidenskabeligt Institut, Copenhagen, 1984.

PRIPP, NINA, *PM till frågan om lagstiftning mot könsdiskriminering*, DS Ju 1975, 7, Stockholm, 1975.

ROBBERSTAD, ANNE, 'En forelesning om kvinnerettslig teori og metode', in *Årbog for Kvinderet*, 1981.

SCHMIDT, FOLKE (ed.), *Discrimination in Employment*, Stockholm, 1978.

SCHLYTER-BERGE, ASTRID, 'Jämställdhetslagen', in *Årbog for Kvinderet*, Copenhagen, 1982.

SKEIE, HEGE, *Likestillingsloven som politisk beslutningsprocess*, Oslo, 1982.

SVERDRUP, TONE, *Lovvern for arbeidstakere i private hjem*, Kvinnerettslige arbeidsnotater No 31, Oslo, 1984.

VALBJØRN, LOTTE, 'Equal Opportunities Consultants in the Danish Public Employment Service', in K. HVIDTFELDT *et al.* (eds), *Strategies for integrating women into the labour market*, Copenhagen, 1982.

WESTERHÄLL-GISSELSON, LOTTA, *Kvinnor och rätt*, Stockholm, 1979.

WIDERBERG, KARIN,
— *Kvinnor, klasser och lagar 1750-1980*, Stockholm, 1980.
— 'Stat och rätt i sexualitetens perspektiv', in *Årbog for Kvinderet*, Copenhagen, 1985.

Yearbook of Women's Law (*Årbog for kvinderet*), 1978-1985, Copenhagen.

9.2 INFORMATION

9.2.1 USEFUL ADDRESSES

Equal Status Council:

Ligestillingsrådet
Tordenskjoldsgade 27
1055 Copenhagen K
Denmark

Ministry of Labour:

Arbejdsministeriet
Laksegade 19
1063 Copenhagen K
Denmark

Confederation of Danish Trade Unions (LO):

Landsorganisationen i Danmark
Rosenørns Allé 12
1634 Copenhagen V
Denmark

Danish Employers' Confederation (DA):

Dansk Arbejdsgiverforening
Vester Voldgade 113
1790 Copenhagen V
Denmark

INDEX